INTERPRETING
SOLAR AND LUNAR RETURNS

A Psychological Approach

Babs Kirby has been a professional astrologer since she gained the Diploma from the Faculty of Astrological Studies in 1984. She is currently Vice President of the Faculty and the Director of the Faculty's Counselling Courses, which she initiated and now teaches. She also teaches certificate and diploma level students for the Faculty, and is a delegate on the Advisory Panel on Astrological Education, as well as being the Press Officer of the newly formed Association of Professional Astrologers. Babs has been involved in Humanistic Psychology since 1972 and has a private psychotherapy practice. She has lectured and run workshops throughout the U.K. and Europe combining humanistic and transpersonal psychology with astrology.

Janey Stubbs studied astrology with the Faculty of Astrological Studies gaining her diploma in 1984 and winning the Margaret Hone award for the best Interpretation Paper. She works as an Astrological Consultant and has taught astrology and run workshops, both individually and with Babs Kirby. She is also a qualified Shiatsu Therapist, working both as a practitioner and a teacher.

INTERPRETING SOLAR AND LUNAR RETURNS

A Psychological Approach

BABS KIRBY AND JANEY STUBBS

Series Editor
STEVE EDDY

ELEMENT BOOKS

© Babs Kirby and Janey Stubbs 1990

First published in Great Britain in 1990 by
Element Books Limited
Longmead, Shaftesbury, Dorset

Cover Illustration by
Janine McNamara

Cover design by
Max Fairbrother

Designed by
Roger Lightfoot

Typeset by Selectmove Ltd, London

Printed and bound in Great Britain
by Billings Ltd, Hylton Road, Worcester

British Library Cataloguing in Publication Data
Kirby, Babs
Interpreting solar and lunar returns : a psychological approach.
1. Astrology
I. Title   II. Stubbs, Janey
133.5

ISBN 1–85230–165–1

CONTENTS

ACKNOWLEDGEMENTS

We would like to thank all those who have helped and encouraged us, both directly and indirectly, in the writing of this book. Our clients, students, colleagues, teachers and friends have all contributed to our understanding of astrology.

In particular we want to thank Mike Harding, for his interest, involvement and support and for running off so many charts for us on his computer; Annabella Kitson for helping with the historical information; Stef Faulkner for the use of her photocopier; Steve Eddy for his support and helpfulness; 'Jack' for allowing us to use his personal story; Eric Clapton for giving Janey his data to use, with a special thanks from Janey for all the inspiration; the AA data services for Steffi Graf's data; the Deutscher Tennis Bund for her whereabouts, and Steffi for just being someone to write about.

Babs would like to thank Marianne Jacoby, for helping her stay steady; Joan Wilmot, for the difference her supervision has made; all her colleagues at the Faculty of Astrological Studies, and especially Sue Tompkins and Lindsay Radermacher for their interest and support; her friends, especially Marie Maguire and Caroline Schofield, and her children Paul Kirby and Rachael Beardshaw, who have each been there for her and borne her unavailability.

Janey would especially like to thank her mother, Gladwys Stubbs, for all her help and support over the years, her son Patrick for his unfailing belief and encouragement, and Krisztina Glausius for her particularly warm and enthusiastic interest.

Finally, we want to thank each other, for it has been with each other we have mainly found support through the struggles and joys of getting this book to publication. As we go to press we have our third house composite Sun opposed by Pluto.

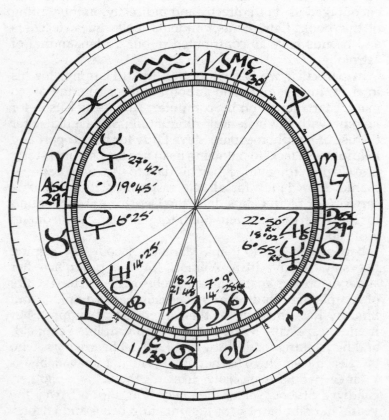

Babs Kirby

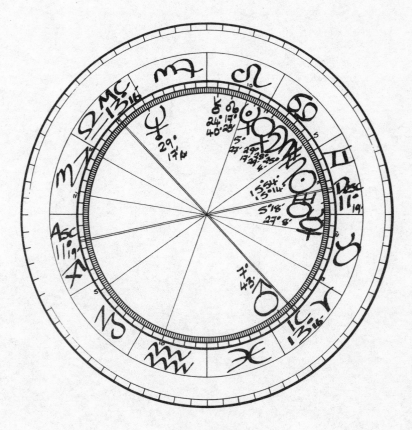

Janey Stubbs

WITH LOVE TO OUR CHILDREN,
PAUL KIRBY, RACHAEL BEARDSHAW
AND PATRICK.

INTRODUCTION

A Solar Return is a chart set up for the exact time the Sun returns to the position it is at in the natal chart. This is always within twenty-four hours of your birthday. Everybody celebrates their birthday and we generally wish one another 'Many Happy Returns', without recognising that it is the Sun's return we are talking about. It is not only people who have birthdays: businesses, organisations and countries also celebrate anniversaries. This book is orientated towards the interpretation of individuals' Solar Returns. The technique to interpret other types of Solar Return is similar, except there will be very little psychological choice and the chart will manifest in a far more literal way.

The Solar Return chart is a unique forecasting tool, giving both a broad overview of the year ahead while also shading in the subtler nuances of experience which may not show up in other forms of predictive astrology.

Solar Returns were very popular in the seventeenth century. Arthur Koestler, on page 426 of his book *The Sleepwalkers* says of Johannes Kepler 'All his life he had been in the habit of casting horoscopes for his birthday.' William Lilly, probably one of the most famous of the English astrologers of that time, would cast a Solar Return when doing detailed case studies and when doing the charts of royal and political people. On pages 734–7 of Lilly's *Christian Astrology* he explains the Solar Return and how to set it up for a given year. Then he works an example by the method of Maginus, giving step-by-step calculations. In his *Catalogue of Astrological Authors* he mentions other sources. Such techniques descended from the Greeks via Arabic and Latin translations which circulated in the West.

In the more recent past, Solar Returns have been mainly used by traditional astrologers in a predictive way. While drawing on some of these traditional ideas, including timing methods, we have developed a psychological and growth-orientated approach to forecasting.

Even if all you ever do with your Solar Return is check out which house the Sun is in for the year ahead, this will tell you something important about the focus and opportunity the year holds. When you have major transits to your Sun, the Solar Return will show at a glance the areas of life you will be engaged with. For example, in her natal chart Janey has a Sun–Saturn conjunction in Gemini in the seventh house. During a year when this was being opposed by transiting Uranus, her Solar Return had the Sun on the IC with Uranus opposing on the MC. Throughout the year she was preoccupied with finding a new home, having just ended a relationship in which the home was shared and also in trying to establish a career as an astrologer. With the Sun conjunct Saturn in Gemini, Janey felt much more secure working with ideas than dealing with the difficult practical matter of finding somewhere to live and so concentrated most of her energy on astrology, which led to her almost becoming homeless. At this point she was forced to recognise that finding somewhere to live must be her priority. The transiting Uranus opposite her seventh house Sun only describes the possibility of a relationship breaking up. But the Solar Return shows very clearly the pull between career and home and the Sun in the fourth indicates that it was vital to concentrate on finding a secure home base in order to have solid foundations on which to build her life.

The more you know of what you are meant to be focusing on, the more you can co-operate with the process you are in and the greater the benefits can be. In client work, you can similarly help your clients to co-operate with destiny. Life hurts most when we fight and resist what is meant. Our Solar Return gives us a wealth of information about the process we are engaged in.

We first became interested in Solar Returns in 1984. Our way into understanding how Solar Returns might work was to look at our own. We started with our current ones, and then proceeded backwards, initially looking at years that stood out as being of particular importance. Eventually we filled in and examined the in between years, to make sure they did not in fact show major significance. From doing workshops we were increasingly requested by clients to do their Solar Return, and we began to look at our clients' Solar Return for our own interest and research. From this, we amassed the ideas that make up this book. A lot of these will be familiar to you, but applied in a slightly different way. From our research, we know that their is no one definitive meaning to any of the chart factors. We have both had very different experiences with similar placements. For this reason we include our own natal charts for your interest. This is our inevitable subjective bias; this is where we are coming from. When you interpret any Solar Return you need to know where the person is coming from, to build your interpretation on your understanding of their natal chart.

Solar Returns fascinated us because they are such a simple way to forecast the year ahead. They give you a tremendous amount of information in a straightforward and accessible form.

We soon became interested in Lunar Returns and what they might hold and tell us in addition to the Solar Return. This is a chart set for the time the Moon returns to its natal position, approximately once a month. Having a computer facilitates this interest, as calculating Lunar Returns is rather a labour of love. However you obtain them, they are well worth it and do describe the months as they go by in a fascinating way. Chapter 7 is a detailed introduction to them and should wet your appetite to start studying yours if you do not already.

This led us into looking at Mercury, Venus and Mars Returns and what they would describe. These are charts set for the time Mercury, Venus and Mars return to their natal positions, approximately once a year with Mercury and Venus, and once every two years with Mars.

The principle in interpreting all Return charts is the same. You take the planet that the Return chart is for, and that becomes the central player, all the other planets within the Return chart are then cast into supporting roles for the main player.

In a Solar Return the Sun has the main role and all the other planets are supporting the solar principle. In a Lunar Return the Moon has the main role, the Lunar Return is telling us about our lunar nature, our feelings, our needs, and how we are on an everyday level. All the planets within a Lunar Return are interpreted within this context. In a Mercury Return the whole chart is describing our mental orientation for the time ahead. All the planets within a Mercury Return add to the picture of how we will be thinking, what we will be discovering and learning. Our Venus Return describes our orientation to relating and pleasure *per se*, and while Venus is the most important planet to interpret within a Venus Return, all the other planets will shade in the more subtle tones. In a Mars Return everything is interpreted within the context of the Mars principle; this provides the framework for the whole chart. This is as yet relatively unexplored astrological territory which we hope others will now feel inspired to take further.

All return charts can help you understand the principle of that particular planet, and how it actually functions (or doesn't) in your life. Any return chart that does not seem to operate indicates that this particular principle is not operating in your life.

When interpreting and using any return chart it is vital to look at the condition of the planet concerned in the natal chart, as well as the natal chart as a whole. The return chart shows the development of a particular planet as it is natally with all its potential and difficulty. Everything within the natal chart is brought along to the return chart which must be interpreted with this in mind. We cannot emphasise enough that the natal chart as a whole must always be referred to, as it is on this that we are building.

1

THE SUN
THROUGH THE HOUSES

Before looking at the interpretation of the Solar Return Sun in the houses, we will stop and consider the principles and meaning of the Sun and what it symbolises in the natal chart and in the Solar Return.

The Sun is the centre of our universe and from it emanate the light and heat that enable all life-forms to exist. It is the heart that pumps out the energy that is essential to life on earth. Without it nothing could live or grow – our planet would be a cold, sterile rock. In the birth chart, therefore, the Sun is the centre and heart which is the source of the essential energy of life. Our vitality and authenticity come from this core. It is the source of our creativity and we must come from it to be true to ourselves and to have real integrity. If this energy is blocked and not being expressed we stagnate and die as people – we are not able to be ourselves. There is a lack of vitality, fulfilment and satisfaction. Nothing matters or seems important and life appears to have no meaning.

The position of the Sun in our birth chart is the key to our essential self, showing how we must seek to integrate our planetary energies in order to achieve wholeness. It symbolises our purest most vital energy from which all growth and creativity spring. By its sign and house the Sun shows how and in what field of activity we will strive to achieve our purpose in life and to become a unique individual. The aspects show how other planetary energies are incorporated into this process.

During its annual journey round the chart, the transiting Sun operates as a spotlight, picking out and emphasising every factor in turn. The Solar Return Chart takes the moment when the natal Sun is in the full glare of the spotlight and reveals to us how the stage is set. It is a picture of the year as a whole, spread out in detail, showing what kinds of experiences and challenges we will undergo and how we will respond to them. The moment the Sun returns to the position of the natal Sun is of great symbolic significance. It is the seed moment of the year ahead.

Because it is focused on the Sun, the Solar Return is a very important guide in the process of individuation. It is telling us how we can best develop the potential of the Sun in any particular year and what we must do to encourage the healthy flow of our solar energy. In this way it is an invaluable tool in helping us to find our path in life, to achieve our purpose and to become more truly ourselves.

The Sun, of course, is the centre and most vital part of the Solar Return chart and its house position is the single most significant factor. The house the Sun is in shows where you are going to achieve your greatest growth. The most important lessons of the year will be met here. It is vital to pay attention to the concerns of this house. If you try to avoid or ignore them then you are likely to be forced to face up to them by events outside your control. You just have to work with these energies as this area is going to be the main focus of attention for the year. It is through working with them that you will develop a stronger sense of your own identity and power.

The Solar Return Sun's house signifies an area where you need to struggle to establish yourself during the year. Through this struggle you get a deeper knowledge of yourself and gain a better understanding of your purpose in life. You develop confidence through meeting the challenges of this house. It is also the area where you can be most creative and gain recognition – you reap the rewards of the energy you put into this sphere of life.

It is here that you battle to overcome obstacles and

become the hero of your own life. It is where you find most satisfaction and fulfilment during that particular year – where you will shine and be noticed.

The Sun in the First House

A year with the Solar Return Sun in the first house is a very important one for self-image. Your sense of identity becomes a major issue as you take a new look at how you see yourself and how you appear to others. You become concerned with yourself as an individual functioning in the world.

When the Sun is in the first you seek a new relationship with your environment and will strive to become more independent – more of an individual. There is a struggle for identity and recognition, a need to be yourself and show yourself as you really are. This year you become more conscious of what you need in life and go all out to get it. You have to learn to put yourself first.

This year is one of positive self-centredness and healthy selfishness as you feel less concerned with others and are able to concentrate on what you need for your own growth and development. If you feel that you are being held back by a restrictive relationship then this is likely to be the year that you have the courage to leave it and go it alone. If it is your job that is impeding progress and self-expression you are likely to want to make a change and find something that is more in tune with your sense of who you are.

It is a year of self-discovery and you may try many different paths before you find the right direction. Growth comes through being daring and experimental as your main purpose this year is to find a means of self-expression which enhances and confirms your identity. In order to do this you need to be open to new ideas and to have the courage to try them out.

It is time for making a fresh start as you have a greater sense of self-awareness and the confidence to go after what you want. Now is the moment for you to shine in the world.

During a year with the Sun in the first you feel vital and alive. There is likely to be a concern with fitness and health and you enjoy being active, getting satisfaction from using your physical energy in new ways. You appreciate being alive.

The Sun in the Second House

When the Solar Return Sun falls into the second house you are called upon to look at your values and question them. What is of true value to you? Is what you are doing in life meaningful to you? You develop a new sense of purpose and look for a path that truly reflects what you believe.

This year you must examine your resources, both at a material level and in terms of the innate talents that you have at your disposal. If you have not been making the most of these then you will be pushed into developing them. Now is the time to capitalise on any opportunities that come your way and it would be advantageous to you to start a training course which refines your natural gifts into marketable skills. It is a time for letting your talents shine out, not for hiding them – for investing your energy productively rather than burying it.

It is also a time for dealing with your material needs – putting your finances in order. You will be forced to grapple with practical issues and must learn how to function effectively in the material world. Money will become an issue, especially if this is an area you have neglected in the past. You are challenged to earn enough to meet your needs. If you are not doing this then you are not free to be yourself. Financial insecurity can weaken your sense of identity and damage your self-esteem. To live in an environment of your own choosing and which truly reflects your tastes and values, enhances your self-image and is a significant factor in your sense of who you are. If these needs are not being provided for then a year with the Sun in the second will bring this to light. You will become aware that you must do something about it. It is time to build a solid and secure base – to lay down firm foundations for your life.

The Sun in the Third House

Communication in its many forms is likely to be the central theme during a year with the Solar Return Sun in the third house. The need to express yourself with words, either spoken or written, becomes a matter of urgency. It is a time for developing and broadening communication skills. You will need to adapt, learn, change and refresh yourself with new ideas, so it is a good year for beginning to study a new subject, going to college, renewing your education – in fact anything that stimulates your mind. You are likely to have a voracious appetite for knowledge this year and will devour books as though your life depended on them.

You will want to be on the go all the time, doing several things at once and will feel very restless with a constant need for activity. The speed of life accelerates and you are able to do much more than usual and will want to whizz around here, there and everywhere!

A change of residence may focus your attention on your immediate locality as you learn to adapt to a new neighbourhood or community causing your sense of identity in a new situation to become an issue.

Brothers and sisters may demand more attention this year and you may be forced to work through some unresolved issues concerning them.

You may need to learn to communicate in a new way – so that you have to think about what you are saying and how you say it. Perhaps you may become involved in a group that is concerned with talking about things in order to understand them or you may start studying something that pushes you to think in a different way and from which a new mode of self-expression develops.

The Sun in the Fourth House

A year that is dominated by the need for emotional security. There is an urgent desire to find a sound base, a home that enhances your identity and enables you to express your individuality more freely. In a year with the Sun in the fourth, getting a mortgage can seem like a gateway to freedom rather than a millstone! Many people choose this time to leave an unsatisfactory relationship in order to find peace and security in a home of their own.

This year is likely to be a turning-point in terms of personal growth and understanding. Attention is drawn inwards and you are able to get in touch with your deepest needs, feelings and memories. It is a time for contemplation and you are going to need plenty of time on your own. Things from the past come to the surface, enabling you to reassess and understand them more fully You are going to be drawn into experiences which require you to draw on your deepest emotional resources and so discover your inner strength.

Your habitual patterns of behaviour too come into question and you are forced to look at them. Old habits can be restrictive and may be getting in the way of self-expression and preventing you from pushing forward in life. There may be a break or change in your normal routines that forces you out of old ruts so that you develop new behaviour patterns that are more appropriate to your present needs.

It is a time when matters concerning your parents or children become an issue so that you have to examine your relationship to them and you may find that you need to make changes there. You feel the need to look back to discover your roots and where you are coming from and this will help you to see more clearly where you need to go from here.

The Sun in the Fifth House

This is a very important year for personal self-expression and fulfilment. There is a drive to make your life what you want it to be, to create your own drama. You want to become the central character in the unfolding story of your life. To this end you throw yourself with passion and enthusiasm into what you do, so that it becomes a true reflection of who you are. There is a need to discover your own inner uniqueness and develop this for your own pleasure and satisfaction. It is a year for taking pride in yourself and for discovering the joy of being yourself.

There will be a challenge to the way in which you actually live life. Are you really using yourself to the full? Are the things that you do really important to you? Do you allow yourself to really enjoy life? Or have you filled your days with duties and obligations that allow you no space or time for play? We tend to see play as an optional extra, not very important, that we fit around the real business of life. But play is an essential part of self-discovery. The things that we do purely for their own sake, because we enjoy doing them, help to develop and strengthen our sense of identity. During a year with the Sun in the fifth then pleasurable activities take on a new meaning and significance. You may find new interests or give more energy to existing ones so that they revitalise you, increasing your self-confidence and enhancing the quality of your life. You get satisfaction out of sport, competition, challenge, and are more able to gamble and take risks. There is a need to pit yourself against life in order to test your strength.

Children too become an issue this year. There is a powerful urge to create and this may take the form either of producing actual children or of giving birth to creative ideas – children of the mind. In either case you are seeking to enhance your identity through recreating something of yourself. Through being with children you may discover and encourage your own inner child so that you are able to be more spontaneous and playful. It is a year when you may have the opportunity to replay your own childhood, perhaps through involvement with children, and heal some of your own early wounds. You are able to give yourself permission to be a child again.

A love affair may bring you a new perspective on yourself. When someone appreciates you and makes you feel special you feel more confident and get an increased sense of your own value. Being in love, too, makes you feel more vital and alive and you feel as though you can do anything. You may literally glow with energy and excitement.

All these different things are a variety of paths which all lead to the discovery of how special and unique you are. You feel a joy in being yourself and in being expressive in a creative way. This is a year in which to develop your gifts, to become someone and for working towards the fulfilment of your inner purpose.

The Sun in the Sixth House

This year is likely to bring your day-to-day work and routines into focus. It is a time for analysing the way you do things, your daily routines, your diet and health-care. You will be called upon to look at how you organise your life. Are your daily routines efficient and realistic? Or do they tend to be self-punishing or forgotten altogether? In other words, does your working life serve you, or are *you* serving *it*? Have you allowed maintaining the structure of your life to become an end in itself rather than a means of supporting your self-expression? If so you may be trapped in a treadmill of purposeless activity which leads to a sense of emptiness and frustration.

During a year with the Sun in the sixth you must sort out a practical way of life which really suits you as an individual. If you have been going against what you really need – living the wrong kind of life-style – then sooner or later this will lead to stress and illness. But illness can be looked upon as a blessing if it forces you to take stock of yourself and the way you live. You will need to ask yourself how you can reorganise your life so that your day-to-day activities and routines are more harmonious and satisfying to you.

It is a time for looking at your working life. Do you value what you do? If your work is unsatisfying you need to look at how you can change it, or your approach to it, in order to make it more fulfilling. Many people feel driven to find a new job when the Sun is in the sixth. There is a need to feel fully involved in your day-to-day work so that you look for something that has a sense of purpose and meaning.

A year with the Sun in the sixth often signifies a complete change of life-style so that the whole rhythm of life is altered. Perhaps you start a new job, become self-employed or retire, or change from being a student to doing a job or vice versa. Sometimes it can be the period after having a baby when a totally different set of routines has to be adjusted to. This is a time for learning to work more effectively, for becoming more aware of your health and taking care of yourself. You may be forced to focus on your health, perhaps through a period of illness and it can be a period of healing.

A year with the Sun in the sixth can be quite a serious time when you feel like working hard and the effort you put into work draws energy from deep within. Often it is a period of preparation and readjustment for a new phase of life to come.

The Sun in the Seventh House

When the Sun is in the seventh house in a Solar Return you find that your energy is focused on learning about yourself through others. This may be through close personal relationships, counselling, any kind of partnership or through open conflict. All these situations give you the opportunity to see yourself mirrored in others and to bounce your self-image off them in order to see yourself more clearly. Parts of yourself that you are afraid of or do not consciously acknowledge are now brought up to the surface as you encounter them in others.

This year will be dominated by your relationships with others and you may become involved in painful struggles as you work through the difficulties you have in close contact with people. Problems are brought out into the open and may cause conflict as you try to sort them out. You become more conscious of your expectations of others and the kind of energy you, yourself, put into relationships. It is a time of reassessment when you become aware of your own contribution rather than blaming the other person for all the difficulties. You learn about how you act in relationships and what you need from them. From this you can see whether you are choosing people who meet these needs and whether you are putting in the necessary effort to make your relationships work. You are likely to find relationships based on dependency unsatisfying and will seek to establish personal interactions which offer a more equal exchange.

This will be a year when you will want to come out into the world, be more public and noticed. It is a time for blossoming out so that you will be looking for opportunities that offer you a more public role and it may signify the beginning of a more dynamic exchange with people in general. You feel the need to be recognised and appreciated by others so that you are likely to want to step into the limelight.

There is an urge to form working partnerships and you will find great satisfaction from working closely with others. You learn a lot from the new perspective that an objective other can give, and you gain confidence in yourself through the experience of supportive co-operation.

The Sun in the Eighth House

This is a year of profound change and transformation during which you experience something that completely alters the direction of your life. It signifies the end of a particular phase of life and the start of a new one. It is a period of rebirth and like birth it may be painful. The metamorphosis may be brought about by an external event such as the loss of someone close or it may be through an inner decision that has far-reaching effects. You may decide to have a child, to begin or end a relationship, or to take a new direction in your career or in your life generally. You feel in the right mood for starting afresh and leaving your old life behind, and you are able to make decisions from which there is no turning back. This is not an easy thing to do and you are likely to be required to dig deep within yourself in order to find the strength to carry out your plans.

With the Sun in the eighth you tend to feel more insular; your feelings are deep and intense, and you may be reluctant to share them. You are going to need a lot of time on your own in order to work through the conflicting emotional insecurities that a time of such drastic change throws up.

Joint finances may become an issue and there may be some sort of crisis around them. This may not necessarily be an actual financial crisis but it could be a change in shared commitments which is symbolic of a deeper change. The question of an inheritance may arise and become a highly charged issue. The money itself may not be important to you as it is the symbolic significance of the gesture that is at stake. You feel the need to be recognised and acknowledged as being a part of something, of being connected. You may receive a windfall at this time which transforms your life and causes an alteration in the way you see yourself – a change in self-concept.

Your sexuality is heightened this year and you may become involved in an obsessive sexual affair or be obsessively attracted to someone unobtainable. Whether or not you become actively engaged in the relationship, your feelings will be deep and all-consuming and will bring to the surface emotions, memories and past hurts that you may have been suppressing for a very long time. You learn a lot about your sexual needs and about your more primitive desires and feelings during a year with the Sun in the eighth, and relationships are likely to be fraught with jealousy and power struggles.

This year may signify the achievement of something that is of such importance to you that it changes your view of yourself from deep inside. You get a greater sense of your own strength and potential and gain a new faith in yourself. During the year you feel a new determination and can be unyieldingly single-minded in working towards your aims. You are able to throw yourself wholeheartedly into what you do and are unwilling to compromise. Through meeting the challenges you face this year you discover a hidden reservoir of strength which will benefit you for the rest of your life.

The Sun in the Ninth House

In a year with the Sun in the ninth you become conscious of the principles by which you live your life and begin to reassess your own philosophy of life. It is a year of increased awareness and personal growth during which you gain a deeper understanding of your own identity, a greater sense of who you are and how you fit into the wider scheme of things.

It is a time when you feel at your most positive and enthusiastic. You have a new optimism and are eager to take fresh opportunities which stretch and broaden you. Some of these new interests and experiences open up whole new areas of life and you may become conscious of a new inner purpose.

There is a search for meaning and the scope of the mind becomes expanded so that your field of activity is greatly increased. At this time you may become deeply interested in a new subject that alters your perspective and changes the way you think.

Travelling to other countries and coming into contact with people from different cultures opens your mind and widens your horizons. You are able to understand more about yourself and the world by becoming aware of other ways of life.

There is a restless thirsting for knowledge and exploration which keeps you constantly on the move. You are open to new and more challenging ideas and there is a need to stretch yourself as you deal with issues outside your normal life. You are no longer able to accept the limitations and constraints that you have made for yourself, so there is an urge to break free and reach out for new experiences.

During a year with the Sun in the ninth you may discover what you truly want to do in life. You feel the need to live by what you really believe in and have enough faith and confidence to do what you intuitively know is right for you even if it seems a gamble. You are able to trust your own judgement and act on it.

The Sun in the Tenth House

This is a very significant year in terms of your identity and image out in the world. You become more aware of the social role you wish to play and the way you want to appear. Your public image becomes more important than usual and you want to be recognised and appreciated for what you do. You want to shine as an individual.

It is a year when reaching an objective or finding a new aim causes a change in your sense of identity. There is a shift in how you see yourself and in how you are perceived by others. This may be brought about through a new career, a promotion or through some other change in social status such as marriage, retirement or becoming a parent.

There is a lot to be sorted out this year as you need to reassess your objectives and to make plans for achieving them. A new direction in life is likely and you are going to be concerned with laying down the groundwork for future success. You may become involved in studying a subject that is directly concerned with advancing your career.

This may be a year when you become conscious of your true vocation in life and find a new purpose in the world. (This is more concrete and outer than the purpose that is found when the Sun is in the ninth house.) Your aims become clearer and more sharply defined and you are filled with a new determination. You will want to go out into the world and find your place by contributing to the community at large. You want to be accepted and acknowledged as an effective and successful person. As you strive for success you are building your confidence and self-esteem and proving to yourself that you are someone of significance.

The Sun in the Eleventh House

This is a year when energy and attention are focused on issues concerned with the wider social group. It is a time for seeking out the company of those who share your ideals and hopes for the future. You need the support of a group who enhance your identity by recognising and fostering your beliefs. With the Sun in the eleventh you want to become a part of something that is moving towards a better future and you are able to set aside your personal ambitions in order to work towards a goal which is concerned with the community at large.

Friendships come under scrutiny as you seek out the company of those who are in harmony with your present aspirations. It is a time of re-evaluation and it is important to be with those who help to strengthen your sense of identity.

You may find yourself being challenged to fit into a new situation. Perhaps you have to learn to live with others by moving in with a group of friends or by becoming part of a community. Or you may find yourself being drawn into working with a group of people. Through these new experiences you learn a lot about yourself and the way in which you interact with others. Through becoming involved in co-operative effort you learn how to maintain your own identity while at the same time being part of a group.

You are also able to discover and develop the talents that you as an individual have to offer the group. At this time you are able to bring a new vitality to collective enterprise and may become the centre of attention, helping to fire others with enthusiasm and inspiring them to give of their best. Because of this you may find yourself becoming the leader or spokesperson for the enterprise or organisation that you are involved in.

During a year with the Sun in the eleventh you look more to the future and put your energy into making your dearest wishes a reality. You develop new ideals and visions and seek to do something that benefits the world as a whole. Your own dreams become identified with a group aim and through this you may enter into a joint creative venture which seeks to make your vision of the future a reality.

The Sun in the Twelfth House

During a year with the Sun in the twelfth you feel an increased need for solitude. You feel more inward-looking and contemplative and will want to retreat from the world and dream. It is hard to be specific about your aims as life seems to be full of infinite possibility. You feel confused about your identity and have a vague yearning to be much more than you are but you do not know exactly what, or how to achieve it. This longing may bring a sense of dissatisfaction so that you could find yourself drifting into escapist activities such as drinking, day-dreaming and watching endless television. You are inclined to be more passive than usual and find it hard to make decisions. You

may even have a feeling of being cut off from the world –
alone and estranged.

It is the end of a cycle and you have reached the
conclusion of a particular phase of life. This embodies
both joy and sadness as you learn to let go of your old life in
order to prepare yourself for the new cycle to come. There is
a need to give something up in order to move on and you
experience the disintegration of old structures as the seed
of the new cycle begins to grow. It is a period of mourning
the past and of understanding your memories. You learn a
lot about yourself by delving into the unconscious and by
listening to what your dreams and fantasies have to say.

You feel more sensitive and impressionable than usual
and are likely to draw great inspiration from music,
poetry or dance. At this time things like meditation and
visualisation techniques are especially beneficial as you
look inwards for answers.

This can also be a time of self-sacrifice and giving to
others and you may become involved in work that is
concerned with caring for people. You feel more sympathetic and altruistic than usual and may be called upon to
give something up for the greater good. Institutions seem
to figure more prominently in your life, either because you
are working or living in one or because you have to spend
a lot of time visiting someone who is.

It is a time when the past catches up with you and you
meet the results of your own actions. Light is thrown on
unfinished business and you will need to clear up any
loose ends. Personal illumination is likely to come through
confinement, dreams and listening to the wisdom of your
unconscious.

2

ASPECTS TO THE SUN

The aspects to the Sun in a Solar Return chart show the kind of qualities and energies that you will be striving to integrate into your identity during the year. You are going to become aware of the need to develop the characteristics of the planet concerned and will make a conscious effort to do so. The planet or planets involved show what it is you need to incorporate and the aspects the way in which this happens.

It is important to bear in mind when looking at a Solar Return that any aspects that you have natally to your Sun are going to affect how you react to that particular year's influences. If, for example, you were born with Sun conjunct Saturn, you will still experience all the self-doubt, caution and lack of confidence that you normally have, even if there is a Sun–Jupiter conjunction in the Solar Return. In fact, a year with a Sun–Jupiter aspect could be a particularly challenging one for you as you are being pushed into letting go of some of your inhibitions and self-limiting notions. Perhaps finding yourself in situations where you have to act spontaneously and take a gamble in order to make the most of new opportunities for growth. If you normally live with Sun–Saturn then you might well feel that you are being pushed along too fast and out of your depth in a year with a Sun–Jupiter aspect. It could also make you feel quite depressed at times as you become aware of just how much you have been limiting yourself in the past. This shows how important it is not to look at the Solar Return aspects in isolation – if you are basically a Saturnian person you will not suddenly become free and easy because Jupiter is conjunct the Sun in this year's Solar Return! But you are going to learn to unbend a little, to take more risks and to develop faith in yourself. You are going to push forward the barriers and perhaps even dispense with some altogether, but it is not likely to be an easy time for you.

Looking at the aspects themselves, a planet conjunct the Sun reflects an internal battle with yourself. You know that you must develop the qualities of the planet but you have to fight against your own reactions, fears and inhibitions to achieve this. Conjunctions represent struggles that have to be resolved – they cannot be avoided.

With the square and the opposition the inner dynamics are the same but the struggle is externalised. The battles you fight tend to be with a concrete adversary, taking the form of conflicts with other people or struggles against difficult circumstances. You feel the need for something outer and tangible to pit yourself against in order to resolve the conflict inside you.

The trine and sextile show changes that are made willingly with the expectation of pleasure. The long-term effect may be just as far-reaching as with the hard aspects but the initial motivation is one of anticipated enjoyment. Even if this hope is not realised it will have made the transition seem much easier.

Aspects from the outer planets to the Sun represent ongoing transits and will appear in several Solar Returns running. They will have most effect when they are nearest to exact and will fall away quite rapidly once the aspect is past, although the after-effects may reverberate for a year or so after this.

Now we will go on to take a more specific look at the Sun in aspect to the other planets in a Solar Return.

Sun–Moon

Aspects between the Sun and the Moon in a Solar Return reflect the search for wholeness and integration. They show how we try to bring together our sense of identity and our emotional needs. Years with aspects between the Sun and Moon will tend to be significant turning-points in your life. If the aspect is a conjunction, opposition or square, the year will be one when the changes are sharply defined and challenging – the years that stand out in your mind when you look back. With the trine and sextile the changes may be just as significant but they are made smoothly and easily so that you do not notice how much you are changing. This is because you are moving with the change rather than having to struggle. You accept the challenge gladly, confident that the experience will be rewarding.

A New Moon in the Solar Return signifies a year of exceptional importance. It is time for a fresh start, a year of awakening when you become consciously aware of your deepest emotional needs and can integrate them with your quest for individuation. You feel at one with yourself and are able to be wholehearted about what you are seeking to achieve. This year you will thrive in the spotlight and need to shine and be recognised for who you are. Success comes through putting yourself heart and soul into what you do. This is not a time for pulling your punches but for going all out for what you want. This applies to any goal whether it is a career ambition or the development of an emotional relationship. During this year your feelings and sense of identity and purpose are brought together, enabling you to throw yourself unreservedly into getting what you need to foster your growth and self-confidence.

A sextile between the Sun and Moon brings an opportunity for personal self-fulfilment and achievement. It can be a very productive time as your emotional needs and sense of identity are functioning in harmony and you get pleasure from putting effort into important objectives.

The Moon square the Sun will be similar to the conjunction except that you have to struggle harder to find yourself. You will have the same desire to bring your feeling nature and your identity together, so that you function more as a whole, but you are forced to fight to achieve this. In order to do this you must break away from old habits and patterns of behaviour which are holding you back. You will have to let go of some of the things that make you feel comfortable and secure in order to bring a new way of life into being. There is a challenge to the structure of everyday life and tensions are brought to a head this year pushing you into making important changes. Anger and resentment that has been suppressed for years will now surface and may be encountered as concrete issues that have to be dealt with.

A year when the Sun is trine the Moon is one when solar and lunar needs are easily combined so that the two operate in harmony and changes can be made easily. It is a time of inner peace and balance when growth and self-understanding can be achieved through quiet contemplation.

During the year you are either preparing for a time of change to come or gaining your equilibrium after a change has been made. It is an opportunity to take a breather, to find your feet and settle into a new routine. You are able to bring your emotional life more into harmony with your search for identity and success which makes it easier to live in a way that is more in tune with your true self. This means that it is likely to be a year of personal happiness and contentment when you feel more at peace with yourself.

With a Full Moon there is an awareness of the need for wholeness and integration and a conscious striving towards achieving this. It symbolises the polarisation of the feelings and the will and during the year an attempt will be made to bring them together. Whether or not this succeeds, a tremendous amount will be learnt about your real needs, both solar and lunar.

During the year you may discover an aim that you

really identify with so that you are able to make a total commitment towards it. You will find satisfaction in completely involving yourself, in making a big effort to realise your goals.

It is a peak time or turning-point when you gain a fresh perspective and begin to move in a new direction. It is a year of maximum objectivity when you are able to see yourself more clearly and gain a new insight into your underlying feelings and motivations. This can be quite uncomfortable and it may be a time of great inner tension as you struggle towards becoming more truly yourself, towards a greater integrity of being.

Sun–Mercury

Only the conjunction is possible and this is likely to be a year of great introspection when you spend a great deal of time thinking, studying and musing – sorting through your thoughts in order to clarify them. You become more concerned with what is going on in your mind and you are likely to be constantly questioning yourself and your motives. Your thinking may tend to be more subjective as you become more strongly identified with your ideas.

Thoughts may be directed inwards through an outer event which brings about a complete change of attitude. This may be through any situation which confines you and throws you in on yourself, causing you to be more contemplative and reflective.

During the year you are likely to receive a challenge to previously held ideas which brings about a rethink. If you have become identified with theories that are no longer relevant to your life and your thinking has become too rigid then something will happen that forces you to adjust your thinking. These newly thought out concepts then become part of your identity.

Sun–Venus

Venus can only form a conjunction, a semi-sextile and a semi-square with the Sun and of these only the conjunction and the semi-square may be powerful enough to make any noticeable impact on your life.

When Venus forms an aspect to the Sun in a Solar Return it often indicates a new relationship or a turning-point in an existing one. You may become more intimately involved with someone you have known for some time or you may make a deeper commitment to an existing partner as the relationship moves in a new direction.

There is a longing to be more connected and closer to people and there may be a rather restless search for friendship and love as you seek out those with whom you can feel a greater sense of harmony and ease. This year you become more aware of what you want from others and so are better able to define your own terms – to make the kind of relationships that are most satisfying to you and which fit your identity.

This is a time when you feel very sociable and enjoy the company of others. You are also likely to feel more inclined to play and enjoy yourself than usual so that it may be a year devoted to the pursuit of pleasure and entertainment. You are more aware of your need to enjoy life and are able to put your own happiness first. It is a year when you can put pleasure before duty.

Venus also often brings rewards, brings you what you most want. So this can be a year when you actually get something that you have been wanting for a long time, something that confirms your identity and makes you feel more uniquely yourself.

Sun–Mars

Sun–Mars aspects occur in years when changes are tackled with zest and enthusiasm. You have the energy and desire to initiate new projects and to go all out for what you want. You are able to throw yourself wholeheartedly into achieving your aims and display a ruthless single-minded determination so that you won't allow anyone or anything to get in your way. This year you are prepared to let everything go except the one thing that you want the most. Your priorities are very clear and you know exactly what is most important to you. You feel more confident and assertive so that you are able to pursue your goals in a more direct and fearless way.

Physical energy is high and you feel restless and impatient. You want to get on with things and get frustrated by delays. Suppressed anger may surface and conflicts are likely to be more frequent and explosive than usual. You are highly volatile and will tend to erupt when you feel you are being blocked or opposed.

This latter tendency will be even more emphasised if the aspect is an opposition. This is a time when you gain confidence and self-knowledge through pitting yourself against others and challenging their ideas and attitudes. You feel the need to assert yourself, battle for what you believe in and force others to see you as an individual. You may find yourself fighting for a cause which helps you to define yourself and you feel brave enough to take on the whole world.

The square too brings an element of self-definition through conflict but the struggle may be against difficult circumstances rather than individuals and you may feel more blocked and frustrated than with the opposition. You have to fight for your sense of identity and it may, at times, seem like a struggle for survival.

With the trine and the sextile you get what you want more easily without having to fight for it. You are able to assert yourself and act swiftly on your decisions. It is a year when you feel confident and strong-willed, so that you are able to make big changes in your life without difficulty. If you have been planning to make a break for some time then this is the year when everything will fall into place and you can make dramatic changes smoothly and easily. You know exactly what you want and are able to act effectively to get it. There is a perfect harmony between what you do and who you are.

Sun–Jupiter

A year with a Sun–Jupiter aspect is a time of great personal development and widening understanding. It is a time to grow through taking risks, meeting challenges and opening up your life so that you gain a new perspective. There is a feeling of restlessness and desire for new experiences which needs to be acted on. If you are too timid and cautious you will feel in a constant state of dissatisfaction which will undermine your confidence. The more new things that you try and the braver you are, the higher your self-esteem will become.

This is going to be a year when you want and expect a lot out of life. There is a feeling of optimism as though anything could be achieved. Because of this it may be a year of extreme highs and lows. There is a tendency with Jupiter aspects to have over-inflated expectations. You are likely to look at this year's Solar Return and think 'Oh great, I'm going to have a wonderful year!' What we often fail to remember is that although Jupiter symbolises growth, we may well be resistant to this and experience growing pains. There is often a feeling of disillusionment and you may feel cheated as reality fails to live up to your expectations and the envisioned wonderful year does not materialise. You may feel a sense of disappointment and failure. You become aware of how your achievements are falling way below your aims and may feel you are getting nowhere. Because so much is wanted, you may not be able to see how much progress you are making and how much you have actually achieved. Generally, though a spirit of optimism and buoyancy will prevail and setbacks are quickly overcome.

It is also going to be a year when you need a great deal of space and freedom, when you feel brave enough to cast aside many of the restrictions that have been limiting you.

Deep down you know exactly what is right for you and will achieve most from listening to your intuition and playing your hunches. It is a time to learn to trust yourself and to act on what your inner voice is telling you. This is a year when you make great strides towards becoming the person that you have always wanted to be.

Sun–Saturn

Years with Sun–Saturn aspects tend to involve hard work and self-discipline. It is a time of constructive action and for putting a lot of effort into getting what you need for yourself. You may be called upon to give up some of your pleasures in order to concentrate on achieving long-term aims. You feel ready to take on new responsibilities and commitments and may choose to buy a house, get married, have a baby, start a more demanding job or study for exams that will help you in your career.

This is a period of re-evaluation and reconstruction and you need to take a long, hard look at yourself and the way you live your life. It will be important for you to sort out what is working for you and what is holding you back. Things that are no longer relevant will have to be allowed to go. So this can be a time of partings and of giving up outworn, self-limiting patterns of behaviour.

During the year you will be pushed into taking life more seriously and forced to grapple with practical matters. It is a time for examining your attitude to money and if this is an area you have been neglecting then you will now have to face up to it. Lack of prudence in the past will catch up with you now and you may find yourself having to deal with financial difficulties. It is time to put your finances in order and put your life on a sound financial footing.

If there are any other areas of life that need attention, then these too will have to be confronted. If you keep running up against the same problems you must ask yourself 'Why?', 'What am I doing wrong?' and 'How can I make constructive changes?' This is a period for sorting

out the practical basis of your life in order to construct a
sound base from which to operate.

Overall, this is a year of learning through experience and
gaining confidence through overcoming difficulties. It is a
time that sees you in a serious frame of mind, when you get
great satisfaction through working hard and shouldering
your responsibilities.

Sun–Uranus

It is difficult to say exactly what might happen with a
Sun–Uranus aspect as the only thing that is certain is
that it won't be what you expect! All your carefully
laid plans are likely to fall apart now and you have to
learn to be flexible and to take the opportunities that
arise. It is a year of sudden changes and unexpected
happenings which may proceed in a rather frustrating
stop/go fashion. There are setbacks and tense times
when nothing moves, followed by sudden bursts of
activity when everything seems to happen at once. This
is an edgy, stressful time when everything you try to do
seems to run into obstructions and difficulties. You feel
in a hurry to make changes and yet find yourself blocked
at every turn. There will be periods when you feel that
you are hanging suspended in mid-air unable to move
in any direction. Then an unexpected opportunity will
suddenly crop up and you are off like a sprinter from the
blocks. Change when it does come is swift and dramatic.
Because of the frustrating waiting periods and the brevity
and speed of the movement you may not realise quite how
drastic and far-reaching the changes you make are. You are
likely to reassess some of your long-term aims and make a
complete change of direction so that this year represents a
significant turning-point in your life.

It is a period when you will want to assert your individuality and develop your own unique talents. You need
the freedom to be yourself and will take swift and decisive
action to get it. Any restrictions will be swept aside in

your drive for greater independence as this year you will have the confidence to act on your own individual ideas. You also feel more detached from other people than usual and therefore better able to do your own thing without regard to the effect it might have on others. In fact, you are likely to get pleasure from shocking others and from appearing eccentric and different this year. To this end you may develop somewhat off-beat ideas and become more rebellious that usual and may become involved in groups which aim to challenge convention and change society. Your identity becomes bound up in Uranian ideals and philosophies as you seek to define yourself more sharply.

Sun–Neptune

Because Neptune moves so slowly a Sun–Neptune aspect will appear in quite a few Solar Returns. It shows a period of restless longing for something beautiful, romantic and glamorous to happen. You yearn for something more than you have and seek out mystical, magical experiences. You have little interest in the mundane and practical but seek to be taken out of this world, to lose yourself, to merge with someone else. You may do this through falling in love, by joining a religious sect or you may turn to drink or drugs to take you out of your everyday life. You are not very clear in your thinking at this time and tend to see things as you want them to be rather than as they are. You will be prone to misjudgements as you reach out and grasp your own illusions. You see only the beauty and potential and brush aside everything that you do not wish to see.

With Sun–Neptune you are learning to let go of rigid concepts and preconceptions. All that seemed solid and secure may now begin to dissolve so that you have to learn to be more accepting, to trust and to let yourself go with the flow of life. You will not be able to hold on to a life-style that is too carefully planned and ordered this year but will be forced to allow things to take their course. Blocks and inhibitions may just melt away, leaving you with a clean sheet on which to start afresh.

This can be a very creative year as you set out to follow your dreams and make them part of your everyday life. You are able to let go of a lot of the things that have been holding you back as you no longer feel much concerned by security and material matters. What you are trying to achieve may seem unrealistic to others but you feel drawn on by the boundless possibilities of life. You are able to make big decisions in a dreamlike trance so that you may not be fully aware of the magnitude of the steps you are taking. This makes it easier for you to carry through changes that you might have been afraid of attempting before.

Sun–Pluto

This aspect indicates many years of profound, trans-formational change, the effects of which will have a very long-lasting effect. Sun–Pluto aspects appear in Solar Returns in years when something really major happens in your life and you are called upon to dig into your deepest resources. This can be a very painful time when you really feel that you are touching rock bottom but, like the Phoenix, you rise again renewed and strengthened. It is the end of a particular phase of life and is usually marked by an experience that touches you deeply such as the birth of a baby, the death of someone close, the end of a relationship or the beginning of a very important one. After this, things will never be the same again.

This can be a period of total dedication as you work compulsively and obsessively towards a personal aim. You feel ruthlessly determined and will bulldoze through anyone or anything that gets in your way. You put all your energy into getting what you want and expect nothing less than total success. Second prize will mean nothing to you now!

During the year your need for power and success is likely to surface and you may be surprised by the depth of your ambition. At times you may feel quite despairing because of the enormity of the task you have set yourself. You want so much that it is hard to know where to begin. Once you have started, however, you will leave no stone unturned in achieving your aim and the force of your desire will enable you to move mountains.

Years with a Sun–Pluto aspect can seem very bleak periods when nothing appears to be moving. You may feel completely blocked, almost paralysed, and this can lead to times of dark depression and despair. But this is a necessary part of Pluto's transforming cycle. It is like winter when everything appears to be dead but under the surface things are beginning to change and grow. It is a time of waiting, of allowing things to take their course in preparation for the spring.

3

INTERPRETING
THE SOLAR RETURN
ASCENDANT AND MIDHEAVEN

The Solar Return Ascendant

The sign on the Ascendant in the Solar Return chart will show the way in which you express yourself during the year and how you appear to others. It will indicate the image you are striving to present to the world in that particular year – how you want to be seen. It will also show how you are going to experience and react to life and the way in which you approach what you do. The Descendant will show how you go about relating to others, what you want from relationships and the sort of people you are likely to be drawn to.

A year that has the same sign rising as your natal Ascendant will be a very significant one in working out the potential of your birth chart, a time when you really blossom forth and come into your own.

If the Solar Return Ascendant falls on a natal planet, then this planet's function is going to be greatly emphasised. For instance, if the Ascendant picks up your natal Mars you will be called upon to learn to deal with your own Mars energy specifically, whereas with Mars rising in the Solar Return it is your general approach to Mars and matters concerning it that will come into focus. The whole subject of the Solar Return Angles picking up natal planets is very important and will be dealt with more fully in Chapter 5.

The natal house that the Solar Return Ascendant falls in

will be in the spotlight during the year and you are likely to experience an emphasis on the concerns of this house. For example, if you have Capricorn rising this year and it falls in your natal second house, you may find that any difficulties that you have with money become an issue. If you normally have a struggle to earn enough for your needs then this will have to be confronted and overcome before you can express yourself freely. So the concerns of the natal house affected underpin your whole approach to life and have to be attended to during the year before you can move forward.

The Ascendant ruler is a very important factor and must be looked at carefully. Its house position will show the area of life that will be the main focus of your self-expression during the year. The sign will show the way in which you can express yourself most effectively and the aspects will indicate how you will tackle the matters of the ruler's house and the sort of experiences and challenges that you are likely to meet in doing this.

A planet on or near the Ascendant will be very significant as it will strongly influence how you perceive life this year and how you project yourself. Because of the impact a rising planet can make it is worth taking a brief look at the effect of each of the outer planets on the Ascendant.

With Jupiter rising in the Solar Return, you will feel much more confident and buoyant than usual and will want to tackle new challenges and take a bit of a gamble in life. Personal freedom will now seem absolutely essential to your self-realisation and you will not be afraid to free yourself from any limiting circumstances. This will be a year when you have enough energy and faith in yourself to leave an outworn relationship, cast off a constricting job and set sail on a voyage of discovery. Life feels full of possibilities and promise.

If Saturn is rising then it will be quite a serious time for you. This is a year when you meet life in a very responsible and self-disciplined way. You will approach new experiences rather cautiously and will want to take life one step at a time. There will be no reckless risk-taking this year. In fact every move you make will be examined from every possible angle before you actually commit yourself to it.

Uranus rising indicates a year of great unpredictability and you may be tempted to make sweeping changes just for the sake of doing something different. You may also have to cope with many unexpected, even shocking, events. There seems to be no pattern to a year with Uranus rising so that you cannot count on anything and have to learn to be very flexible. During the year you will want to accentuate your independence and originality and may behave in a very eccentric way. Others will find you hard to understand as you constantly change direction. Because you need to feel completely free to act on the spur of the moment you will totally avoid anything that feels like a long-term commitment.

If Neptune is on the Ascendant you are going to be approaching life in a very dreamy and romantic way, seeing the best in everyone and being very receptive and impressionable. It will be a time when you let go of your defences and feel the need to be at one with the universe. You will tend to be somewhat gullible and may be swept off your feet by someone glamorous and charismatic or be drawn to those in need of help in some way – falling in love with an alcoholic, perhaps, and imagining you can 'save' them! Neptune rising in a Solar Return generally signifies a time of transition when your whole approach to life is going through a period of metamorphosis. You will be letting go of your old ways of interacting with the world in order to be free to redefine yourself. You may encounter new people or situations that cause you to question yourself so that you feel very confused about who you are and how you appear to others. It is a time of trial and error.

Pluto rising means a year of total transformation. People or experiences that you encounter this year will have a profound effect on you and how you see yourself and you may be pulled down into something very deep and dark. You will be brought up against yourself and forced to face up to buried feelings and motivations that shock you to the core. There will be times when you really feel as though your back is against the wall and that you have reached the limits of your endurance. This may be a very dark night but when the day dawns you will be born afresh.

The Sign on the Ascendant

Aries Rising

This is a year in which self-assertion and independence become an issue. You will want to define yourself more clearly and will push ahead with your plans regardless of what others think. It is a time when you feel very positive and active, you know exactly what you want and have the self-belief to go for it.

During the year you are likely to develop many fresh interests and start numerous new projects. Now is the moment to be daring and experimental, to have a go at anything that attracts your attention. You will learn a lot by testing yourself in new situations and gain confidence through meeting challenges head on.

A year with Aries rising marks the beginning of a new cycle in life. It signifies a time to start afresh, when you are able to see yourself in a completely new light and can tackle the world with renewed vigour and courage.

Taurus Rising

When Taurus is rising in your Solar Return you will be more concerned with living in the present than with future aims. You will be happy to let yourself simply be who you are and to live by your own values. This enables you to take quite major decisions and carry them through without it seeming such a big thing. Perhaps you have been planning to do something for years but have never had the courage to do it and this year you just do it easily and effortlessly. This is because you are focused on here and now, so that you want life to be happy and satisfying at this moment in time rather than dreaming of a rosy future. It is a year when you feel sufficiently secure and sure of yourself to make your life what you want it to be. This then is going to be a year of concrete action when you do what has to be done, with quiet determination.

There will be an emphasis on the physical as you become more in touch with your body and its needs. You feel more sensual and are likely to be more sexually active than usual and will also enjoy treating yourself to healthy pleasures like massage and saunas.

Gemini Rising

The Ascendant in Gemini in a Solar Return indicates a year when communication is likely to be of paramount importance. If you have previously been rather shy and retiring, you may now suddenly emerge from the background as you feel an urgent need to talk to people, to exchange ideas and to learn. You may develop new interests and become involved in intellectual activities that were of no interest to you previously. It is a time for experimenting with new ways of self-expression and you may develop skills in writing, public speaking or teaching. You will feel intellectually curious and will seek to increase your knowledge of the world through reading, listening and studying.

Generally it will be a year of many changes and much movement. You will want to do many different things and go to a variety of places. This is a year when you learn to become more adaptable and versatile and during this time you will learn a lot that will be useful to you in the future.

At this time you will feel very sociable and friendly. There will be an urge to make mental connections with people, to talk to them and to learn about them. You want to know what makes people tick and how they think. Your approach to life, this year, is lively and light-hearted and you have an insatiable curiosity which gives you a genuine interest in others and makes making friends easier than usual.

Cancer Rising

With Cancer rising you will tend to feel more inward-looking. There is a need to retreat from the world and spend more time alone. You will want to feel safe, secure and emotionally nurtured so it will be important for you to feel good about your surroundings and to be in tune with those around you.

This can be a very creative time but activities are likely to be centred on the home. You may find that you want to make changes to your environment or you could become involved in a project that involves working or studying at home.

There will be a focus on matters concerning your home and you may move house or set up a home with someone. Finding or creating the kind of home you want is part of your self-expression this year.

You may also tend to feel more vulnerable than usual and to feel things more deeply. You are likely to feel soft and exposed and so will want to be with people that you feel safe with. You will also be more receptive and responsive to other people and more sensitive to their needs, which means that they are likely to seek you out for emotional support.

Leo Rising

A Solar Return with Leo rising indicates that this is going to be a very important year for you as an individual. It is likely to be a year when you step into the limelight and thrive on attention – you make your presence felt.

Your creative energy will be high and can be used to good effect. It is a time for developing your own special talents and for being authentic and true to yourself. What you do is likely to be appreciated by others and you may gain some sort of recognition.

This year your sense of identity will be strong and you will be able to concentrate your energy on your own personal needs. Your energy level and vitality should be high and you will be able to tackle life with vigour and determination. The house the Sun is in will show the area where you need to focus your energy and in which you want to shine and be recognised.

Virgo Rising

Virgo rising generally signifies a year of learning and study. You may become interested in something new and want to learn all you can about it. You will approach your studies seriously and will want them to have a practical aim, such as developing and enhancing your career or training for a new one. It can also be a time when you actually change jobs and have to learn new skills and new ways of doing things. In some way you will be learning new things which affect your daily routines and work so that you have to learn to be more flexible.

You are likely to develop a more conscientious and responsible approach to life, gaining satisfaction from working hard and doing the right thing. You will get on with what has to be done, in a methodical and efficient way.

It is a time of preparation and reorganising yourself for a new phase of life to come. Your self-image is going through a period of change and you are learning skills that will help you to become more yourself.

Libra Rising

Libra rising indicates a year when shared experiences and relationships become of foremost importance to you. There will be a need for closer relationships which may either be friendship or love but which will definitely mean learning about yourself through others. Working partnerships, too, are likely to be more important this year and you will find special satisfaction from working with another person.

It is a year of much social activity and you may become involved in groups, particularly those which help you to understand yourself through dialogue or counselling. You feel the need for greater social interaction and companionship as you look for people who enhance your sense of who you are by sharing your ideas and interests.

This will be a time when you will want to create a harmonious environment for yourself both by beautifying your physical environment and by seeking out people you feel attuned to. Your aesthetic sense is likely to be heightened so that you become more appreciative of art and beauty.

Scorpio Rising

A year with Scorpio rising is likely to be one of profound experience and deep emotion. Changes are likely to occur which alter your view of yourself for ever. There will be an intensity in the way you go about things and you throw yourself wholeheartedly into what you do and pursue your aims with single-minded determination. You are likely to feel an inner compulsion to make drastic changes in yourself which transform the whole way you approach life.

This is likely to be a year in which you end one phase of your life and begin another. It is a period of rebirth when you emerge as a completely new person. But first you have to go deep into yourself, so that it is a good time for therapy, for digging up what is hidden and bringing it to light. Your feelings will be deep and intense and you need to spend time focusing on your inner life and discovering emotions and experiences that have been suppressed and buried. It is a time to acknowledge and understand the darker, more instinctual side of your nature.

Sagittarius Rising

This is likely to be a restless, exciting year when you feel the urge to travel and explore. There will be a thirst for new experience which drives you on to take more risks than usual. This is a time for breaking free and for doing things that you have never dared to do before.

You will want to travel both physically and in your mind and may make many journeys. It is a year of expanding horizons and forward momentum. Things suddenly seem possible and you may make a move that opens up your whole life. You feel stimulated by challenges and will seek out new ones once you have reached one goal. At the moment you will be more concerned with the quality of the journey than in getting there! It is a year when you look outward towards the future and grow stronger through being daring and casting aside some of the shackles that have been binding you. You will want a great deal of freedom and space this year!

Capricorn Rising

When Capricorn is rising in the Solar Return, you are likely to experience a year of achievement through effort. It will be a time when duty and hard work come first and you are capable of great self-discipline. You feel a new sense of responsibility for yourself and will want to have full control over the direction of your life.

This year you will be able to tackle the most daunting tasks and work in a very constructive and effective way. You may take on projects and initiate schemes which involve a lot of work for you but you get a deep sense of satisfaction from doing this.

The impression you make on the world may become an issue to you and you are likely to be concerned with your image and how you present yourself.

Everything you do this year will be done for a purpose and you gladly take on new responsibilities. You are able to commit yourself fully to what you do and approach everything in a very determined and conscientious way. If you really want something you will be prepared to work slowly and carefully towards getting it, however long it takes.

Aquarius Rising

During a year with Aquarius rising you will feel a new sense of independence. You will not want to be confined by conventional structures and will set about liberating yourself from them. Personal freedom will become a priority for you and you will want to live by your own beliefs. Your appearance too will reflect your desire to express yourself as you really are so that you may become more nonconformist in the way you dress, even perhaps adopting a somewhat eccentric style. You will be asserting your uniqueness and forcing people to look at you in a new way.

This is likely to be a year when close relationships are less in focus as you will be more concerned with wider issues. There will be a need to share your ideals with like-minded people and you could become involved in groups which aim to change society.

During the year you will redefine the way you relate to the world. It is a time when old patterns will be broken down and new ones established. It is a time of focusing on the future and putting your energy into long-term aspirations.

Pisces Rising

A Solar Return with Pisces rising indicates a year when you feel more sensitive, mystical and dreamy than usual and you will be drawn into experiences that feed the spiritual side of your nature. It is a time of learning to let go, to allow things to happen which are outside your control and you will find that you cannot make things happen by force. You just have to surrender power and trust that you will get what you need.

It is a time when you may be called upon to be many different things to many different people and your understanding of yourself deepens through having to adapt to the needs of others. There may be some degree of self-sacrifice involved as you may find yourself in a position where you have to look after other people. You will tend to feel great compassion and sympathy for people in need and will willingly give your time to help them.

The image that you present to others this year may be rather confusing as, rather like a chameleon, you change to suit the situation so that you are never quite the same from one moment to the next. You are in the process of developing a new image and first have to let go of your present definition of yourself which may be too rigidly confining. It is a year when your self-imposed boundaries dissolve and you are able to open yourself up to the world and feel at one with it.

The Solar Return Midheaven

The Midheaven in the Solar Return chart shows what qualities you will want to develop during the year and what you are most likely to be consciously striving for. It describes what your expectations are and your status in the community. It is an indication of what your purpose and direction are likely to be during the coming year. It shows how you will be seen and how you want to be seen, what you will show of yourself to the world and what your orientation will be. The shift in consciousness that any Solar Return Midheaven brings will become part of your growth and unfoldment. Although this Midheaven will only last for a year, it is a new part of yourself that you will discover and actualise during that year and which will be incorporated and built upon in the following years. The Solar Return Midheaven shows how you become conscious of your solar needs.

The house of the Midheaven ruler will show in what field you will seek to realise your long-term objectives and the kind of opportunities you will seek to create to fulfil your ambitions. It shows more specifically the task of the year ahead. For example, with the MC ruler in the eight house your task for the year will be that of inner transformation and change. You would be aiming to seek a deeper intimacy with others and learning to share yourself in a more profound and meaningful way so that relationships become catalysts in your transmogrification.

The Sign on the Midheaven

Aries Midheaven

With Aries on the Midheaven you will want to put over a public image of decisiveness and self-reliance. Your goals for the year will be concerned with establishing your independence and you will want to aim towards becoming your own boss.

Taurus Midheaven

During a year with Taurus on the Midheaven you will feel the need to build something permanent and secure. Your main objective is to create a stable and solid base right now and you will not be looking too far ahead. At this time you will want to project an image of being reliable and trustworthy and it will be important to you that people recognise and respect you for these qualities.

Gemini Midheaven

When Gemini is on the Midheaven you will be concerned with finding a niche in life that allows you more scope for communicating your own ideas. You may look for a career that allows more freedom of self-expression and more contact with people. You are likely to feel very restless this year and may explore several long-term aims as you become more easily bored than usual and find it hard to concentrate on one goal for very long.

Cancer Midheaven

A year with Cancer on the Midheaven will be a time when you need to feel emotionally involved with your career and you will seek long-term goals which enable you to protect and nurture others in some way. You will be searching for a place in the world that feels right to you and where you feel at home. This year you will want to be seen as someone who is caring and concerned.

Leo Midheaven

With Leo on the Midheaven you will be striving towards discovering a vocation that truly expresses who you are – something that draws on your creative energy. Your aim this year is to be yourself and if, in the past, you have been acting against your real needs, then this is a time to put this right. If your work does not fit your identity you will take steps to change it now. It will be important to you to appear authentic and honest, someone to be admired and respected for who you are.

Virgo Midheaven

Virgo on the Midheaven indicates a year when you will find satisfaction through working hard and conscientiously. You will want to appear to be perfect and may set yourself impossibly high standards. There may be a tendency to become bogged down in detail so that it is difficult for you to see very far ahead. It is a time for analysing and re-evaluating your goals and defining them more specifically.

Libra Midheaven

A year with Libra on the Midheaven is a time when your aim will be to find balance and harmony in your life. There will be a need to work in partnership and share your goals and achievements with another person. You will want to spread peace and mutual understanding and will look for an occupation that enables you to do this. This year you will want to be appreciated for your ability to get on with people and it will be important to you that people like you, so that you are likely to make a special effort to please others.

Scorpio Midheaven

When Scorpio is on the Midheaven you are likely to have a single-minded obsessiveness about achieving your aims. You throw yourself into working for what you want with intensity and passion and will want total involvement. There will be a need for you to be involved in work or projects that have a deeply transforming effect on you, on other people, or on the environment.

Sagittarius Midheaven

With Sagittarius on the Midheaven you are going to be looking far into the future. This is a time for setting far-reaching goals because having something meaningful to aim for will be much more important to you than what you actually achieve. You may feel an urge to work in other countries or to travel as part of your work and you will want to spread your knowledge and understanding far and wide.

Capricorn Midheaven

Capricorn on the Midheaven signifies a year of solid ambition and determination. Your goals will now be strictly realistic and practical. You know exactly what you want to achieve and work patiently and persistently to get there. This year you will want to be recognised for your hard work and social responsibility. It will be important to you to succeed through the established channels of your profession and the acknowledgement of your achievements by those in authority will be very important to you.

Aquarius Midheaven

This is a time of idealism when you will want to work with your ideas and hopes for the future. It is a year of group effort and social aims, when concern for the world in general will seem to be more important than personal ambition. At this time it will be important to you that your work allows you to express your own unique ideas freely and you will want to be in a position where you can make innovative changes.

Pisces Midheaven

With Pisces on the Midheaven it is going to be a year when
it is hard to find a definite direction. You feel a yearning
to do something special and yet you may find yourself
awash with confusion as you search for a more spiritually
orientated direction. This year there seems to be an infinite
choice of possibilities and you may feel overwhelmed by
it all. It is time to let go of aims which are too rigid and
confining as you search for a place in the world that reflects
your inner truth.

4

THE MOON IN
THE SOLAR RETURN

The Moon in the Solar Return shows, by house, what area of life will be emphasised on a feeling and day-to-day level, and by sign, the mode in which a person will respond.

The Moon fluctuates and its house position will show the area of life where changes will occur and hence where events will take place. By progressing the Moon, approximately 1 degree a month, events can be predicted as the Moon makes exact aspects to other planets in the Solar Return chart and in the natal chart; although not everything will necessarily manifest externally and some events may only be felt and experienced on an inner level. Chapter 6 gives details of how to calculate the progressed Moon exactly, and the case study in Chapter 9 demonstrates how to work with it.

The Moon also shows a person's relationship with the public and their public image, something that is more important for those in the public eye but which can also be important for business people and for anyone dealing with the public in any capacity.

The Moon shows relationship needs, particularly feeling and emotional needs, and the way significant relationships are formed.

The Moon shows by its sign, the type of emotional contact we need in order to feel nurtured, and how we will go about getting that, and by its house, the area of life where we have emotional needs and want to feel secure, where we want to feel accepted and at home.

In a Solar Return the Moon's function is in describing and meeting emotional needs which in turn support the solar principle. For example, with the Moon in the fourth house, the Moon indicates the need to establish a secure base within yourself, in order to be yourself, which the Sun will describe. A fourth house Moon describes what has to be attended to this year in order to venture out into the world and express the solar principle. The more you are secure within yourself, the more able you are to express yourself.

What follows are some suggestions of how the Moon might be experienced through the signs and houses. These are intended to stimulate your own thinking, bearing in mind that within a Solar Return the Moon is at all times playing a supporting role in relation to the Sun.

The Moon through the Signs

The Moon in Aries

This is a year of being direct and straightforward in your emotional reactions and responses to people and situations. It is not a year for tact or diplomacy or for keeping a cool head as your responses will be faster and more spontaneous than usual. At times you may wish you had counted to ten before you said what you felt, but this is a period when you tend to blurt things out. The main benefit from this will be a clarity and honesty between yourself and others that you can really trust and feel secure in. Others may describe you as being like a 'breath of fresh air'.

This is a good time for you to take the initiative in relationships and to make new contacts with others in general. You will be taking bigger risks with how you feel, as you are feeling braver about exposing and sharing your inner world; you could make quite an impact. Your intuition is heightened so it is a good time to trust your hunches.

The Moon in Taurus

With the Moon in Taurus you would expect a year when your need for stability and security is more keenly felt than usual. There is a need for calm and emotional steadiness.

There may well be strong sensual needs, which if thwarted could lead to an inclination to eat too much rich food and gain weight. Alternatively a need to eat simply and wholesomely might be felt. It is a time to pay attention to your body. If you have ever considered having a regular massage, or visiting the Turkish baths, you would particularly enjoy and benefit from it now.

It might be a period when you would feel nourished by gardening, by growing things, and by being in the countryside and with nature.

The Moon in Gemini

There will be a need to communicate, a need to understand and to relate through an exchange of ideas.

This is a time when you may develop diverse interests as you are at your most curious. You will feel at home in the world of ideas and thought. You may have to grapple with uncomfortable feelings within yourself regarding your mental ability. This could be through attempting to do something that stretches you mentally.

With the Moon in Gemini your emotions change quickly and you are prone to boredom; you need plenty of stimulation. This is a restless period, a time when you need movement both mentally and physically. It is a good idea to establish as flexible a schedule as your life will allow.

You may want to talk about your feelings, to analyse, to dissect, in order to gain a greater understanding of your inner world.

The Moon in Cancer

A year with the Moon in Cancer will accentuate the need to feel close to others. A need to belong, on a very personal level, as well as on a more global level, is emphasised. There is a need to feel that you are a part of a whole, where and how you fit in, to feel your connectedness to others and to life generally. This could be a time of review and readjustment regarding your place within your family and background.

There is a need to nurture and be nurtured. All your personal relationships are emphasised this year and depending on how satisfactory they are this could be a time of change and adjustment while you attempt to improve things. You are more in touch with your own needs for closeness and relatedness and as a consequence you may feel more vulnerable.

This is a year when you are at your most in touch with your more primitive and instinctual knowledge of life. In your relating to the world you will be more inclined to act and to respond from your instincts and you will have a good sense of how others feel. Your instinctual understanding is working well.

The Moon in Leo

With the Moon in Leo it is a year when being able to express yourself will be important. In particular, your emotional responses and reactions will be on display and will enhance your sense of authenticity and significance. This is a year when you will want a lot of attention and recognition, you will want to feel of significance, and you may enjoy being in the limelight. It is a time to do something that will warrant the attention you crave and that will give you a sense of pride in yourself.

You may feel moved to be more creative in your life, not necessarily artistically unless you are ordinarily an artist, but more in everyday ways.

The Moon in Virgo

This will be a year in which you are looking at the particular and the parts of situations, and of your life, in order to get a sense of the overall pattern. You will be needing to make sense of the hows and whys of your day-to-day existence. You may be creating more order in your day-to-day life. You may be concerned with your health, diet, sleep patterns and fitness, restructuring your life so it is healthier and more whole. This is time to introspect and analyse and see how things work for you, to implement a new routine that accords with your own personal patterns and reflects your own person.

The Moon in Libra

There is a need for partnership and one-to-one relating, mainly of a personal kind but possibly professional as well. You are likely to want to relate through an exchange of ideas. It is a time of feeling open and friendly towards others, and of being particularly tactful, diplomatic, charming and gracious. Romantic involvements are emphasised and you may bring more romance into existing relationships.

You may wish to make yourself or your home more beautiful. With yourself, this could be a time when you have a lot more interest than usual in new clothes and new styles, and in decorating yourself with make-up or jewellery. Within your home you could want to change the decoration and furnishings in a similar way to enhance its beauty.

There will be a need for peace and harmony within your home and yet there may be considerable discord and disruption in your attempts to achieve this. This could leave you feeling jarred and pained and demand a lot of your energy to resolve.

In general your aesthetic sensitivity is enhanced and you may feel drawn to and nurtured by any involvement in the arts and want to extend and develop your artistic, musical and literary interests.

The Moon in Scorpio

There is a need for intensity and meaning when the Moon is in Scorpio. You are likely to desire a deep feeling connection to someone which is likely to have a powerful and transforming effect on you. You will be taking your feelings very seriously and trying to understand yourself. This is both a profound and complicated time emotionally for you, with the possibility of intense moods as you are more prone to keep your feelings very private and bottled up inside yourself.

You may find yourself in a financial partnership, which may or may not be beneficial, but which leads you subsequently into strong feelings within yourself relating to the whole arrangement.

The overriding need of this year is to connect to your own emotional depths, and this is most likely to happen through a passionate involvement.

The Moon in Sagittarius

This is a year when there will be a need for freedom and adventure. Your curiosity about life and your zest for living is high. Your urge to discover and explore is at its greatest. This could manifest in an external way and lead you to travel; pilgrimages to far-distant places. This is a very literal way of expanding your everyday horizons.

Or it could manifest on a more inward and psychological level and lead you towards a greater interest in 'things of ultimate concern', like philosophy and religions and the meaning of life.

Whether or not you travel, you may make contacts or connections with foreign people or people who open you up to a fresh way of looking at life. In all your relating you will want adventure and freedom. You are likely to be blunt and to-the-point and you are at your most extroverted.

You may feel a particular need for wide-open expanses of countryside and feel particularly nurtured by time spent roaming in unspoilt areas of natural beauty. Your idealism is strong and you will have an optimistic faith in the essential goodness of the world.

The Moon in Capricorn

With the Moon in Capricorn there will be a need for structure and order in your life. You are likely to be reserved and self-contained emotionally, being fairly cautious and realistic in relation to others. Practical considerations may at times be more important and pressing than your emotional needs. Your judgement of others is particularly astute and accurate and you have an acceptance and tolerance of the realities of life.

You may have a strong sense of what you want to achieve, of what your goals and ambitions in life are. You may feel the lack of a position and status if you have not achieved what you would have wished. You may find you are looking for your position in life through a relationship, particularly if you are a woman, and need to review if this does in fact give you what you want. There may need to be a reconciliation between career goals and more personal needs, the need for a career being a very strong force this year.

The Moon in Aquarius

If the Moon is in Aquarius there will be a need for independence and autonomy. You will want to do your own thing and in your own way. You may want to experiment with your life-style. You may have a radical overhaul of your domestic situation and instigate new codes of behaviour and an egalitarian rota for chores. It is a time when you are more aware of your beliefs and ideals. They will influence your day-to-day life and may lead you to effect changes in your life-style.

Group activities may be prominent this year as you will feel a need to find your place within groups. You may feel particularly at home in a group, or find a group to which you feel you belong. It is likely to be a time when you are more sociable generally, meeting and relating to a greater diversity of people.

The Moon in Pisces

This will be a year of enhanced sensitivity and feeling. You will be especially sympathetic and compassionate in all your relating. There will be a yearning for oneness and for merging which could lead to a lack of boundaries between you and others. At the highest level you will be seeking a mystical, spiritual connection, but this could result in a muddled confusion of not quite knowing where you begin and others end. You may indulge in a lot of day-dreaming and fantasy and find mundane and material matters trying. It is a good time for meditation and you will naturally be inclined to contemplation. You are longing for something magical and may be able to inject something magical into your everyday life.

It is a time when any artistic and creative talents that you have will be accentuated. You will be more receptive to your creative urges and feel nourished either by being creative yourself or by appreciating the creative efforts of others.

The Moon through the Houses

The Moon in the First House

With the Moon in the first house your feelings will be more visible to others. You are likely to be aware of and show more vulnerability. You may appear inconstant to others as the fluctuations in your feelings are more obvious. You may feel very exposed, as if your inner world has become an open book.

It is a good time for making sympathetic contact with others. Your responses are immediate and sincere and will make you appear accessible.

There is also likely to be an increased sensitivity to your environment, and to the atmosphere in your surroundings.

The Moon in the Second House

This is a year in which your need for security will be felt strongly. This may manifest as a need for emotional or material security. You may get to understand how your finances affect your well-being on a feeling level. It may be a good year for acquiring money, you have an instinct for it. This is particularly true of a second house fire Moon.

What is of value to you emotionally is emphasised this year and it may be that you will discover a deeper set of values and a clearer sense of what you really need. You may also have a clearer sense of what you have within you that is of value to others, what you have to give which could give you a greater sense of security.

Your own feelings are likely to be steadfast and loyal, possibly possessive of those you love in whom you have invested your security.

The Moon in the Third House

A year in which your need for mental stimulation will be accentuated. You may feel restless and find it difficult to settle, feeling easily distracted by a variety of interests. You could be studying yourself, possibly literally at home, or you could feel very 'at home' studying. You could also be teaching, and again this could be literally classes you teach in your home.

There may be some changes in your neighbourhood or local community which affect how you fit into it. It could be that you have actually moved recently and this year is concerned with getting to know your new neighbourhood, setting up new routines and relationships, and generally establishing your place in your local community. For those who have not moved, community issues may be of more concern to you throughout this year.

If you have any difficulties ordinarily with a brother or sister, then this could be something you will become concerned by and attempt to put in order throughout the year.

In all the possible scenarios discussed you will be concerned with sorting out what you need emotionally in order to function.

The Moon in the Fourth House

This will be an introspective year, a time for quiet contemplation and reflection, maybe reviewing your past and your childhood and family. This could be an appropriate time for some kind of counselling or therapy, if that is something you have ever considered, since you will be engaged in a process of unravelling some of your early conditioning anyway.

This is a year in which you will want to spend a lot of time at home, enjoying your privacy. You will have a need for time alone.

This is a time too of getting your home circumstances right, possibly a time for making changes in your home. You need your home to be a place to which you can retreat, where you feel safe and emotionally supported; a place which nurtures and replenishes you. In so far as your home does not fulfil this function, the year could involve considerable adjustments in an attempt to create a safe and secure base. It is a year in which your most basic and fundamental security needs are being emphasised.

The Moon in the Fifth House

With the Moon in the fifth house there will be an emphasis on expressing how you feel. Letting others know how you feel will be your way of saying 'This is me; this is who I am.' You will be at your most emotionally dramatic. Even if you would normally never make scenes, this is a year when you might, and if you are someone who does then this year will be full of them.

It could be a romantically important time, love affairs and falling in and out of love occupying you a great deal. You could feel as if you are on an emotional rollercoaster. This is a year in which the pleasure principle is emphasised. You may enjoy theatre visits and parties where you get a lot of attention and the potential for romance hovers.

It could also be a time in which you feel particularly creative, possibly on a domestic level, or in some creative project that engages you emotionally.

The Moon in the Sixth House

This is a time in which work is emphasised. You may be working particularly hard on something that grips and absorbs you. Your moods and feeling fluxes will be linked closely with your work routines and efficiency, so that at times your feeling state may inhibit your effectiveness. It might also be that within your working sphere people around you are increasingly turning to you as someone to confide in and discuss their emotional problems with, and that you become known as someone with a sympathetic ear. It is important that you do not become overloaded yourself as your own health and well-being could then be at risk.

It is also a time to understand the importance of things like your daily personal routines, rituals and rhythms of life. You are more likely now to be able to fine-tune your daily existence so you function at an optimum level. You will experience more directly the links between eating healthily, having a regular sleep pattern and getting enough exercise, and your capacity to function efficiently and feel good.

The Moon in the Seventh House

This is a year in which relationships are emphasised. If you are not in a serious relationship then trying to find someone may be a priority for you this year. You are going to be more open than usual to forming a partnership and more aware of your own needs for a relationship. If you are already in a relationship this could mean, if your needs are being met, that you feel particularly happy and content and that being with your partner is a priority. It could also mean, if your needs are not being met, that you will be focusing on improving your relationship so that it satisfies you more fully.

Business partnerships would also be affected, the emphasis being on how well you get along and give each other what you need.

All friendships may fluctuate and change as you move through a process of establishing them on a stronger footing, and making them work better for you. What you need from others is being emphasised and you are open to making more of an effort to sort this area of your life out.

It could mean that certain friendships that no longer work for you will be left behind and new people will come into your life.

The Moon in the Eighth House

Intimacy is emphasised in a year with the Solar Return Moon in the eighth house. If in your life you do not have much intimacy with anyone, if you do not share your inner world within either a close relationship or close friendship then this year may feel particularly lonely and painful as you grapple with the emptiness. You will be prepared to risk more to obtain deeper contact with those you know and will gain a great deal of satisfaction and security from sharing more of yourself. Those who do have satisfactory relationships and friendships will still be likely to be strengthening and improving them and discovering new personal dimensions through intimate contact.

A new relationship could start, and if so it is likely to be particularly deep, significant and transforming.

The Moon in the Ninth House

The Moon in the Ninth house indicates a year in which travel or study could play an important part. You might travel and find your spiritual home, you might feel very comfortable and at home within another culture. This may teach you something about your own emotional make-up. You may not travel, but still feel drawn to knowing people from other cultures and be fascinated by their differences.

You may feel at home studying; particularly subjects that broaden your horizons and teach you more about life, such as languages, and religious and philosophical subjects. You might be plunged into new feeling depths within yourself through something you are studying. This could either be through the subject matter, or through the study situation.

You may want more freedom and scope to experiment in all your relating. It is a year where 'the meaning of life' concerns you and you are trying to find your particular place in the grand scheme.

The Moon in the Tenth House

This will be a period in which your status and standing within the community is emphasised. You may be in the public eye more than usual. It could be a time when you enjoy a lot of attention on a public level, when you are seen.

You are particularly well tuned in to what the public needs and wants right now, so it is a good time for launching a new product or new idea. You have a sense of the pulse of the moment, so now is a good time for both business and personal advancement.

You are likely to be going through a process of adjustment and reconciliation to the position you have achieved so far within your life. As a result you could be having various feelings about your success or lack of it and you will be aware of what you would like to have achieved and be known for.

On a psychological level you are potentially able to develop an understanding of how your mother's unconscious ambitions may be influencing you, and to separate out what you might be living out for her, and what you really want for yourself. So it is a good time to discover more of what you want for yourself on a professional level.

The Moon in the Eleventh House

Friendships and social activities are emphasised in a year with the Moon in the eleventh house. You are likely to feel more sociable generally and to be widening your circle of friends.

You may join a group of some sort or become more involved with one you already belong to. Knowing, discovering and establishing your place within all groups you are associated with will be an important experience this year. From this you will deepen your self-awareness and gain emotional confidence and security.

You may feel moved to involve yourself in idealistically motivated projects. These may be based on long-held but dormant ideals, or new ideals forming. Wishes and longings you may have held for a long time are being awakened at this time and you are likely to make moves towards fulfilling them.

The Moon in the Twelfth House

With the Moon in the twelfth house your main preoccupation will be with your most private life and inner world. This will be a year in which you will need time to be alone, to reflect and contemplate. This is a good time to take up meditation, to write a journal or keep a dream diary. Pay attention to your inner stirrings and listen to the messages from your unconscious and allow yourself to be guided by them to a wholer existence. This is a good time for any artistic expression that comes from an inner attunement. This is also a good year for spiritual development. If solitude and privacy are threatening to you then you could feel lonely and isolated a lot of the time. This is because turning inwards is difficult for you, in which case you may try to escape through various ways, excessively watching television, or using alcohol and drugs being possibilities. If you find yourself in this predicament you might consider obtaining some guidance, as you are losing your way.

You may feel more of a link with others in lonely or difficult circumstances and involve yourself in a helping capacity. This can be a constructive route towards recognising your own inner difficulties, which you find reflected in others, although you may not realise your own identification and personal investment at first.

Aspects to the Moon

The aspects to the Solar Return Moon, both from the natal chart and within the Solar Return chart, and the aspects you have in your natal chart to your natal Moon, are all going to influence the functioning of the Moon in any given year.

If you have a Moon–Saturn conjunction natally, even if you have a Moon–Uranus conjunction in Sagittarius one year, there is still going to be a background influence of the natal Moon–Saturn conjunction. So while you may have a comparatively wild, expansive, freedom-orientated year, you will still have a sense of the caution and emotional carefulness that is an ever-present factor in your personality. The conjunction to Uranus may bring out the tendency to go cold and frozen on situations, to feel highly strung, tense and generally anxious. It could be that this year will wake you up to realising how generally anxious you are on an everyday level and you may well grow a lot emotionally.

This is just one example of how complicated it can be to talk about aspects in isolation when in fact there are always several aspects plus the natal predisposition to consider. We will look at all of this in more detail in the case studies, but as you use these sections bear all this in mind and see how the various aspects might combine.

In all the descriptions on aspects I am describing just the bringing together of the two principles involved and, again, you must adjust this depending on whether the aspect is challenging or flowing. Within a Solar Return difficult aspects will not signify the kind of pain and difficulty that they might within a natal chart. When an aspect echoes an existing difficulty within you this provides an opportunity to make progress within yourself regarding this issue. When there is a difficult aspect within the Solar Return that does not have any echoes within the natal chart, then you can expect the more positive manifestation of this aspect. Challenging aspects tend to show our more concrete experiences, whereas the flowing aspects tend to show things we take for granted and do not particularly notice.

Moon–Mercury

The effects of this contact will be similar to the Moon in Gemini and probably fairly subtle. It is a year when you may want to communicate your feelings and are also inclined to try to rationalise how you feel. It is a year in which both communication and understanding are emphasised. You may be analysing yourself and your responses.

Your mind is likely to be especially alert and open to new ways of seeing things. It is a good time to write and for all kinds of communication. Making contact with others on a mind level is emphasised, both profound and ordinary.

It is a good time for imaginative thinking. Your ideas could be very subjective and your feeling states could be influencing your ideas, which could be useful for any ideas based on personal experience.

Moon–Venus

With the Moon and Venus in aspect then relationships are emphasised and likely to be auspicious. Friendships may bring gain, harmony, love, money, happiness, peace and fulfilment, and good contacts and relationships with women are likely for both sexes. If the Moon and Venus are in a challenging aspect there is a possibility that relationships will be unhappy, as there is conflict within you regarding what you want which creates dissatisfaction emotionally. This is a good time to try to reconcile inner conflicts and an opportunity to find a personal resolution to long-standing relationship issues.

Moon–Mars

The effect of this contact is similar to the Moon in Aries. Both the expression of your feelings and the likelihood of taking action based on how you feel is emphasised. You are likely to be more emotionally volatile and to be more outspoken, speaking your mind frankly. You may be too impulsive and hasty at times, rather reckless and impatient. You could also be argumentative and headstrong. This is a time where 'fools rush in where angels fear to tread', and you are liable to put your foot in it by responding impulsively without having first thought things through and weighed up what you want to say. This is a good time for the timid to be braver, for the shy to come out of their shells and be less self-conscious, and for being more emotionally authentic and making genuine spontaneous contact.

Moon–Jupiter

With the Moon in aspect to Jupiter an expansive time emotionally is emphasised. You want a feeling of growth and freedom and of reaching out for new emotional experiences that stretch you. You will have a lot of optimism and hope and a sense of future possibilities. New opportunities will come your way for expansion.

There may be grandiose plans and a tendency to inflate or be pompous. There can also be a tendency to grow/inflate physically, so watch your weight unless you want to put some on. Be careful not to go overboard on the good life, extravagance being a distinct possibility. You are prone to over-stretching yourself and feeling frazzled as a consequence, and of being generally unrealistic and extremely restless. You are also prone to being over-generous and promising more than you can deliver.

More positively, there may be a sense of protection, of guardian angels on your side. Your luck is running high and hunches pay off. If the Moon and Jupiter are in a hard aspect, your intuition is less reliable, but you still have a faith and confidence that stands you in good stead.

Moon–Saturn

You are likely to feel constrained emotionally, somewhat shy and self-conscious. You may find yourself in a new situation in which you feel socially awkward and uncom-fortable and you may feel anxious about relating. This is a year in which any new friendships formed are likely to be deep and important and will probably last a long time; you will be very bound to each other. However, you may be quite lonely and introspective this year, finding it difficult to make satifying contact and preferring to be alone.

It is an important time for balancing professional de-mands with personal needs and according each enough time in your life. If your life is lop-sided in this respect then you will be restructuring things to bring about a better balance for your total well-being. Sometimes this will mean reassessing existing friendships to see how well they still serve and satisfy your needs, as you will be ready to recognise if they have gone stale or got stuck in a rut. So if friendships end now it may be good to let them go and something better will emerge, either with the same person or someone new. It could be that if you ordinarily give a lot to others you may want to hold back and conserve your energy for yourself. It may mean you withdraw for a time as you reassess things and rediscover your priorities.

Moon–Uranus

With the Moon in aspect to Uranus a time of emotional awakening is emphasised. What you are awakened to will depend on what house your Solar Return Moon occupies as well as the condition of your natal Moon. Awakenings often come in the form of events. Something from outside befalls us and we are jolted out of ourselves. With the Moon it will be something habitual and everyday that is disturbed. It means you need to wake up to something and have perhaps become complacent in certain areas. So it is likely to be an exciting time, with unpredictable things happening, especially on a relating level and within your personal life.

It is a year when you may make friendships with unusual people, people you would not normally be socially connected to. You are more prone to acting on impulse and suddenly upping and doing something. It is likely to be quite an eventful year, with plenty of surprises and changes. You are definitely likely to be much changed by the end of it.

Issues concerning personal freedom or women's freedom could arise. If you are not already sympathetic to feminism or social oppression, you may become more so this year.

You may literally sleep less this year and your energy is likely to be more keyed up and frenetic. Uranus can have a splitting-off effect so you will be less grounded in your feelings than usual. It could also be that you will reconnect to past feelings that you have been split off from and numb to. This would mean painful feelings emerging, but it could bring you greater wholeness and depth and trust in your life.

Moon–Neptune

A Moon–Neptune aspect in a Solar Return signifies a year with a similar tone to the Moon in Pisces or the twelfth house. Your imagination and sensitivity are emphasised and you are likely to have a lot of sympathy, empathy and kindliness for others.

There is often a lack of clarity on a feeling level: so much is possible and there is no sense of boundaries. There may be a lot of confusion about what in fact you do feel. There is going to be a strong pull to merge with others. At its highest level this is a spiritual yearning for oneness with the divine. On a more prosaic level it can mean losing yourself or becoming confused and disorientated. You may crave something magical, something out of this world. You will do a lot to inject some magic into your everyday life and at times it may be as if you have been touched by something magical, and then moments of sheer bliss are experienced.

These are essentially mystical experiences and you may be more open to a mystical or spiritual understanding of life during this time. In your longing for something ideal, however, you are also prone to being taken in by illusions and wishful thinking. You are open to deception and to feeling disillusioned and disappointed by life. You are at your most gullible.

If you are involved in any artistic or creative work then this could be a particularly productive time for you as your artistic faculties are heightened. Your fantasy and dream world is likely to be active and satisfaction can be derived from creating your own works of art, from participating in artistic activities, or from appreciating the arts.

Moon–Pluto

With the Moon in aspect to Pluto in the Solar Return then a year of emotional depth and intensity is emphasised. There will be similarities to an eighth house Moon and a Moon in Scorpio.

Pluto rules what is unconscious, buried and inaccessible and when it contacts the Moon then habits based on early family conditions and feelings buried in childhood may bubble up to the surface and there may be emotional eruptions. There may also be times during the year when you feel stagnant and inert, as if nothing is happening and you feel especially dead and depressed, yet from this a new phase will emerge with greater awareness.

You may find yourself involved in a power struggle with a woman, and as a result get in touch with less conscious parts of yourself.

A new relationship may begin that is complicated in some way and through the issues this throws up you will develop a deeper emotional knowledge of yourself. An existing relationship may go through a particularly bumpy patch which again teaches you more about yourself on a feeling level. Moon–Pluto contacts, particularly the hard aspects, tend to bring extremes. You may find yourself involved in an intense and passionate relationship, or isolated and alone. In both situations you will be discovering more about your needs and inner world.

This is also a year when you are likely to make radical changes and to be dissatisfied with any aspect of your everyday life and personal life that is not going well for you. You have a great capacity to bring about positive and far-reaching changes. For a woman this could also be extended to how she looks and how she identifies herself. Again these changes will spring from dissatisfaction and the process of bringing about changes may include a certain amount of despair and depression. It is from these rather dark times that a new life breaks through. The more you resist change and try to hang on to a clearly unsatisfactory situation, the more painful this time can be, as you will be blocking the opportunity for new things to emerge. Something must die for the next phase to be born.

5

OTHER CONSIDERATIONS IN INTERPRETING SOLAR RETURNS

In this chapter we will look at how to weigh up and begin to synthesise the various factors in a Solar Return, and at how to interpret the aspects between the Solar Return and the natal chart. We will start by discussing the significance of the remaining personal planets, Mercury, Venus and Mars, in the Solar Return chart.

Mercury represents the way you learn, think, perceive and communicate and in the Solar Return it is significant in terms of its sign, house and aspects. The sign shows the way you think about subjects and shows how you learn, your approach to it. Mercury will frequently be found in the same sign in the Solar Return as it occupies in the natal chart. This is always significant, as this will show whether you are operating mentally in a familiar mode or in a way that is not as familiar to you and therefore stretches your mind. If Mercury is in the same sign as the Sun this can indicate you are primarily learning about yourself.

The house Mercury is in will show the area of life you are going to learn about and what your mind is going to be preoccupied with. It will show your motivation for learning. For instance with Mercury in the eighth house you might learn more thoroughly, or you might develop an intense sexual interest through learning, or that might be your motivation to learn.

Aspects to Mercury within the Solar Return can be interpreted in a similar way to natal aspects, bearing in mind that this is something that is experienced for just one year and the deeper and more negative psychological issues are not going to manifest from this. You can, by and large, interpret aspects in a fairly optimistic and positive light, unless there are other factors that support a particular difficulty. So conjunctions, squares and oppositions will tend to create something concrete and tangible that is obvious as an issue in your life throughout the year but these aspects will not be distressing and problematic in the way they can be within the natal chart.

Venus in the Solar Return describes by sign the way in which we relate and need to be related to. It will show what we want from relationships now, possibly what we lack and what we have become aware of that we have not got. For instance if Venus is in Cancer there is a need to be with people you feel a strong attunement to, people you are at one with in a non-verbal way. There is a need for ordinary, everyday companionship where no effort has to be made to relate – the taken for granted, silently presented cup of tea. Depending on whether or not you have this level of companionship the year could be very contented and fulfilled or distressing and lonely as you realise how much you miss it. If you do not have enough companionship the year will focus on improving your situation. The aspects to Venus will describe how easy or difficult this process will be.

Like Mercury, Venus is frequently going to be in the same sign in the Solar Return as it is in the natal chart. It, too, is then 'at home' and its principle is operating in a familiar way. There is an ease during these years, whereas when Venus is in a different sign there is more of a challenge in expressing its principle. If Venus is in the same sign as the Sun then love and relatedness may be concerned with the realisation and expression of your individuality, or love may stimulate identity issues.

Venus' house will show the areas of life from which will be derived most pleasure and happiness. For example with Venus in the fifth house you might want to have fun and enjoy parties and flirtations.

Aspects to Venus, similarly to Mercury, need interpreting with a light touch and in a constructive way. For example Saturn conjunct Venus in the Solar Return often means a commitment within a relationship. Love is serious. The more difficult components of Saturn–Venus will not manifest solely from this contact.

Mars in the Solar Return shows, by sign, the way you assert yourself; the way you go about doing things.

Mars will show, by its house position, the area of life you assert yourself in. It shows where you actually do things. The area of life the house describes will be the focus of your energy. It could also be an area of conflict.

The aspects will modify the expression of Mars' principles. They will flavour and colour the way Mars manifests. For example a Mars–Neptune conjunction in Capricorn in the second house might be someone who puts a tremendous amount of energy and work into fulfilling a dream. It could be a time of great inspiration to achieve something they believe in, using inner talents, and potentially earning them a lot of money. They will feel enhanced from their success, and be more aware of their own inner resources.

The case studies in Chapters 9,10 and 11 demonstrate further how to interpret and synthesise the Solar Return.

Aspects between Solar Return Planets and the Natal Chart

Contacts between planets in the Solar Return chart with the planets and Angles in the natal chart are highly significant, particularly when aspect patterns are being contacted in the natal chart. We give a small orb, maximum 3 degrees, and focus on conjunctions, squares and oppositions. To interpret these it is essential to have a thorough grasp of the main themes in the natal chart as this is what you are building on. The greater your basic understanding of the way the principles in the natal chart work then the clearer the picture of the year ahead you will be able to build. With a Solar Return chart you are in some ways using similar techniques to those used in synastry, only with a Solar Return you are comparing the influences to a particular person from the cosmos for the coming year. In making the chart comparison a lot of thought is needed to take into account where the person is coming from, that is, their natal chart.

We will outline some of the effects of aspects between Solar Return planets and natal chart planets. These effects can often be quite subtle and not immediately obvious, operating beneath the surface and underpinning the more obvious effects. Our interpretations will always need modifying and personalising when being interpreted with regard to the natal chart as a whole and the Solar Return chart as a whole. We hope you can use what we say as a stimulus for your own thinking.

The Solar Return planet shows the channel of expression for that year while the natal planet shows the backdrop influence that the Solar Return planet is drawing on.

Contacts to the Natal Chart Moon from the Solar Return

Any planet in the Solar Return chart falling on the natal Moon will have, as a background influence, all that the Moon symbolises. This will mean that your feeling nature and instinctual responses will be the source from which the Solar Return planet's expression will derive.

Contacts between the Solar Return Moon and natal Moon are especially significant, indicating a year in which your inner sense of security and well-being is emphasised. How 'at home and okay' you feel in yourself and in the world will be at issue and you will see the results of this reflected in your life. Depending on how far you are able to get your needs met, which shows how much you accept yourself, this time will be a rewarding and happy time or a time when important lessons around self-acceptance are learned.

If it is the Solar Return Mercury that aspects the natal Moon then you may want to talk about, analyse or reflect on your feelings, habits and emotional responses. Your ideas are likely to be subjective. You may write imaginatively.

Aspects from the Solar Return Venus to the natal Moon indicate that your security needs are going to be your main criteria in all your relating. Friendships and partnerships will be valued according to how well, or not, they satisfy your emotional needs. You will be sympathetic and responsive to others yourself.

Solar Return Mars contacting the natal Moon may mean you will be prone to emotional outbursts. Mars energy is rash and impulsive, and will be expressing the Moon's principles, which are instinctual, habitual and security-orientated. It could be you will assert (Mars) yourself more within your home (Moon). You are more able to ask for things that you need that enhance your feelings of safety and inner well-being.

Mars also symbolises your sexual energy. This indicates that your needs for emotional safety and security will be the source from which your sexual drive will emanate. Your sexual nature and feeling nature are combining, and if they are ordinarily more split within you, then this could be a year in which you will feel both more vulnerable and more emotionally involved in your sexual relating.

When it is one of the slower-moving planets in the Solar Return that contacts your natal Moon then this is a transit to your natal Moon which can be interpreted in the usual way, with the additional information of the houses occupied in the Solar Return chart, which show more specifically which areas of life will be affected by this transit in the coming year.

If the natal Moon conjuncts the Solar Return Ascendant then there will be an immediacy to how you react to situations, your feeling responses will be very visible, and you may feel quite vulnerable and exposed at times. It is a good time for making genuine contact with others as you will also be at your most sympathetic and empathetic, and will in turn draw these responses from others.

With the natal Moon conjunct the IC of the Solar Return your inner security needs are of prime importance and you will be at your most private and inaccessible, wanting to keep your personal life to yourself and those you feel safe with. It is a time of 'holing up', either alone or with someone you are intimate with. It is a time to reflect on and understand the past and early family influences.

The Solar Return Descendant conjunct the natal Moon may increase your need of and dependency on others. You will be more sensitive in all your relating and the feeling rapport between you and all friends will matter to you a lot. For those in the public eye this can be a good time for popularity.

Natal Moon on the Solar Return MC is an excellent contact for business success and public exposure. On a personal level your main concerns will be around your career and goals in life.

Contacts to the Natal Chart Mercury from the Solar Return

Any planet in the Solar Return chart that falls on natal Mercury will have as a backdrop a need to communicate, to think and to analyse.

If the Solar Return Moon aspects natal Mercury then it is a good time for presenting your ideas, opinions and beliefs persuasively. It is an optimum time for you to be well received, as you are receptive to others and how they are receiving you and can modify your presentation accordingly. This is a good contact for creative communication of all types and will be especially helpful to those who work in any of those areas. All Moon–Mercury combinations are good for imaginative writing.

Solar Return Mercury conjunct natal Mercury indicates a year when you can express your ideas in a mode that is comfortable to you. Your mind is working well, you can reach your own ideas and bring them forward.

With Solar Return Venus contacting natal Mercury you

might expect to feel pleasure and happiness in expressing the principles of natal Mercury. You might enjoy writing, feel happy thinking and reflecting, communicating and exchanging ideas. You are going to feel happy using your mind and relating through ideas.

Mars in the Solar Return in aspect to natal Mercury usually means that you will be asserting your opinions. This is a good time for pushing forward with your ideas, and for telling people what you really think and for all types of forceful and dynamic communication. This is not a good year for tact or diplomacy as you will be more impetuous than usual; it is a good time for verbal and athletic competition and where any swift, accurate action is called for.

With the Solar Return Ascendent conjunct natal Mercury you will be outspoken with your ideas and opinions and it will be more important for you to just say what you think. You may write as a way of expressing your ideas.

Natal Mercury conjunct the Solar Return IC will indicate a time of inner reflection on your past, possibly an interest in your ancestry. You will be keeping your thoughts and opinions rather private. It could indicate a time to write at home.

The Solar Return Descendant conjunct natal Mercury indicates that an exchange of ideas with friends and partners is important during this time. All communication with others is emphasised. For those involved in communication professionally this is a good time for progress, as you will be listened to.

With natal Mercury on the Solar Return MC you are likely to be involved in communicating out into the world in some way. This could be literally, through public speaking or it could be through some form of teaching or instruction. Linking and exchanging are emphasised so it is a good time for travelling around within a familiar region and for trading.

Contacts to the Natal Chart Venus from the Solar Return

Natal Venus contacted by Solar Return planets gives a backdrop influence of charm, consideration and relatedness, acceptance, pleasure and relaxation.

With the Solar Return Moon in contact with Venus then there is a great capacity for happiness, peace and fulfilment and good relationships. You will be responding to people with charm and love and will attract favourable responses in return. You will be feeling happier within yourself.

Solar Return Mercury in aspect to natal Venus indicates that you will come to understand your love nature better over the course of the year. You are likely to be more articulate about what you want and about what is of value to you. You will be able to communicate in a pleasing and harmonious way. It could be a time in which you express yourself artistically.

When Solar Return Venus aspects natal Venus then you will be relating in a familiar mode. You are at your most attractive and surer of yourself as a result. There will be an ease in relating and an emphasis on socialising. It is a time when you are at one with your love nature, and friendships and partnerships are auspicious.

If ordinarily you are preoccupied with material concerns, this will also be emphasised this year.

Solar Return Mars in contact to natal Venus could mean you have a rare gift in being able to assert yourself in a harmonious and charming way, 'winning ways' as it were. This is a time when you will have a lot of sex appeal and come across in a charismatic way. This is a very good year for being popular, especially with those who might find you sexually attractive.

With the Solar Return Ascendant conjunct natal Venus you will be showing your most attractive side, at your most accommodating, and concerned that life runs smoothly and harmoniously. You will be occupied with relationships.

With the IC of the Solar Return conjunct natal Venus

you will be concerned with the harmony of your most private and personal life. You will enjoy being at home in comfortable and familiar surroundings, possibly entertaining more than you usually do.

If natal Venus is conjunct the Solar Return Descendant you will be concerned with friendships and all your relating. You will seek harmonious and pleasurable times with others; this could be a very sociable time. Depending on what your existing situation is with regard to intimate partnership, there may be various developments as personal happiness in a love relationship will be a priority for you throughout this year.

Natal Venus conjunct the Solar Return MC indicates a time in which you are more likely to find the world a beautiful place and to radiate happiness and contentment. It could also indicate material good fortune. For those involved professionally in creative and artistic careers this is a particularly fortunate time when you will receive rewards and recognition.

Contacts to the Natal Chart Mars from the Solar Return

Natal Mars contacted by Solar Return planets gives a background influence of assertion, drive, will and sexual energy. It will make a planet more dynamic, courageous, active, possibly competitive and impatient with a lot of energy and charge behind its expression.

If the Solar Return Moon aspects natal Mars you might expect emotional outbursts and shows of temper. There is a charge to your feeling nature and both feelings and emotions will be hotter and more passionate. You are also likely to be franker and more outspoken about personal needs.

When Mercury in the Solar Return aspects natal Mars you may be able to understand better the things that make you angry and reflect on the reasons behind your reactions. You will be better able to discuss frustrations and to assert yourself in general.

If the Solar Return Venus makes this contact you might expect a strong sexual desire or passionate love interest during the year. You are likely to be demanding (Mars) acceptance (Venus); to have an aggressive (Mars) charm (Venus); to be winning (Mars) affection (Venus). Your competitive side is being given an acceptable and charming face, which can get you a long way as those around are likely to be disarmed.

With natal Mars aspecting the Solar Return Mars your familiar mode of asserting yourself and of going about doing things is stimulated and intensified. Depending on the aspect, either you will be spurred on to attempt new activities that test your courage or you may feel more confident and certain of yourself and as a consequence tackle more daring enterprises. Either way your energy level will be high.

Natal Mars conjunct the Solar Return Ascendant indicates you will be showing your most competitive side. What you are competing for will depend on other factors, but it is likely you will be making an impact and being noticed. This is a self-assertive time that you can propel you forward. It is a good time for taking risks as you will enjoy challenge.

When the Solar Return IC conjuncts natal Mars then your capacity to assert yourself is directed inwards. You are at your most private regarding things that anger or annoy you, not letting others know. You own actions may be more subversive, with you acting in indirect and subtle ways. It is a good time for taking psychological risks and for acting powerfully in emotional situations. It could mean you assert yourself at home.

The Solar Return Descendant conjunct natal Mars indicates heated and passionate interactions with others, and is especially good for sexual relationships. You will want to assert your differences in all your close relating. This could indicate rows. It is a good time for all competitive activities, both physical and mental. Tennis or squash would be ideal.

Natal Mars conjunct the Solar Return MC will indicate a

year in which you will be asserting yourself in the world and making your mark. A good time for taking professional risks, as you are at your most courageous and daring and any changes and enterprises you initiate stand a very good chance of success.

Contacts to the Natal Chart Jupiter from the Solar Return

If a planet in the Solar Return chart contacts natal Jupiter then the expression of the planet's principles will be expanded; there will be growth, possibly inflation and exaggeration in how its principle manifests. There will be an opportunity for something new to develop. There may be an increase in philosophical understanding or religious interest and awareness in general, depending on how your natal Jupiter manifests in your life normally, and which planet in the Solar Return is contacting it. There may be luck and good fortune from hunches paying off, as your intuition is working well.

The Solar Return Moon in contact to natal Jupiter shows a sense of protection and an easy expression of the feelings. This is a year of emotional richness and abundance. You will be particularly generous, supportive and warm-hearted and will find others responding to you in these ways too.

Natal Jupiter aspected by the Solar Return Mercury indicates that your mind will be particularly active and curious and that mental stimulation will be a priority. Your thinking may become more philosophical. You may feel restless, and you will need a lot of movement, possibly physical movement like dance or tai chi, or travel to new places of interest.

With the Solar Return Venus contacting natal Jupiter your capacity to love is increased. This contact gives you the potential to realise a lot of happiness any satisfaction in your personal life. It can also magnify any dissatisfactions you feel, and incline you to roam in search of improvements in your love-life. This will be sociable time.

With Venus–Jupiter contacts your sense of well-being is enhanced; you are likely to feel more relaxed than you usually do, with a tendency to over-indulge. When found in earth signs in particular this can indicate a weight gain, so unless this is something you want you will need to be careful about this tendency.

These contacts can also be fortunate where money is concerned, indicating an increase in income. They also indicate you will be spending more and living at a more luxurious level. You may find you spend more than you gain.

With the Solar Return Mars contacting natal Jupiter you might take far more risks, either physically or psychologically. You will be pitting yourself against any obstacles you encounter and will be willing to challenge life to the utmost and risk all. Luck will probably be on your side, so you can afford to take chances. You will thrive on the excitement. You are not likely to have much patience, and will not feel good in situations that require this. You are at your most loud and flamboyant, so anything that calls for this you will excel at.

If natal Jupiter conjuncts the Solar Return Ascendant, the normal operation of the Jupiter principle in your life will be on the surface and very visible. It will mean you will be showing your most optimistic and expansive side and that you will appear very positive and confident. You may also display a more philosophical outlook. You may feel restless, with a need to stretch yourself in various ways, possibly mentally through studying or physically through travel to new places.

With the Solar Return IC conjunct natal Jupiter you will want to grow and expand in private and personal ways. This could manifest literally as a move to a bigger house, or a need for wide open spaces to roam, or it could be that you will venture into previously unexplored psychological territory; your inner space (IC) being expanded (Jupiter).

Natal Jupiter conjunct the Solar Return Descendant indicates good fortune in your contact with others. You will be generous yourself and will draw others' generosity to you. You may meet someone who teaches you something important, or you may yourself be teaching others. You may meet a foreign person, or be drawn to a foreign culture, which similarly teaches you important lessons.

If the Solar Return MC conjuncts natal Jupiter then the direction of your year will be Jupiterean. It is an indication of an opportunity for something new to start with regard to your overall direction in life. This could mean mean new opportunities to develop your career, or your goals in life may change. You are likely to be branching out in some way. It is likely to be a fortunate year, with lucky breaks which you must seize and build on if you do not want them to be just a 'flash in the pan'.

Contacts to the Natal Chart Saturn from the Solar Return

When a planet in the Solar Return chart is contacting natal Saturn there will be a structuring and consolidating of the planet's energy.

The principle of the Solar Return planet will become concentrated and serious, with a feeling of being restricted or limited. Your sense of responsibility, of obligation and duty will be constellated and expressed by the principles of the Solar Return planet.

You will want to gain control and mastery of that area of expression and there will be a sense of restraint and discipline and hard work. There may be ambition and the desire to achieve and attain something.

Things from your past may also surface in connection to the planet that is the channel for Saturn; with the Moon childhood, with Venus old loves, and be reflected upon.

There is work to be done and the expression of the planet's energy demands your review and take stock of yourself and get it working better for you.

With the Solar Return Moon aspecting natal Saturn then your emotional expression is likely to be inhibited and you are likely to feel shy and socially awkward. You may want to spend time alone, being more introspective. Light and superficial contact will not satisfy you at this time and could leave you feeling lonely and alienated. This is a time when you take your inner security and well-being seriously and you need any contact you have to be deep and meaningful.

If the Solar Return Mercury aspects Saturn then your mind is capable of great concentration. It is a good time for study for examinations. Your thinking is disciplined, serious, logical and profound. There is the capacity for much insight.

Solar Return Venus in aspect to natal Saturn may mean you make a commitment in a relationship. You may be more vulnerable and introspective in any existing relationships. Love is more serious, and you are more likely to want to formalise any informal arrangements. It is a time when depth, loyalty and commitment in all friendships is emphasised.

Mars in the Solar Return in aspect to natal Saturn will focus your drive. You will be clearer about where you are going and what you want and extremely determined in your efforts to achieve your goals. Your mode of action will be slower and more concentrated, and you will be more capable of sustained and enduring hard work.

Natal Saturn conjunct the Ascendant of the Solar Return indicates that you will be presenting your more serious and cautious side to the world. You may feel exposed and vulnerable as your inner fears and insecurities surface and become more visible. You will feel that everyone can see how ill-equipped you feel to deal with various situations and you will find yourself confronted by those very things that you feel least able to deal with. You will in fact manage everything very well and it can be an extremely important time for establishing a deeper inner strength and security based on a realistic knowledge of your capabilities.

The Solar Return IC conjunct natal Saturn indicates a deeply introspective time. You will want a lot of privacy. You will feel acutely any lack of security in your most personal and private life and it is a good time to take steps to establish solid foundations. This might take the outer form of buying land or a home, or making necessary repairs to an existing home.

With natal Saturn conjunct the Descendant you will be reviewing all your friendships and relationships to see how well they work for you, and any that are not working may come to an end. You want things to work, and bring stringent criteria to bear. In other respects this can feel similar to Solar Return Venus contacting natal Saturn, with issues involving commitment, responsibility and obligation within relationships especially emphasised.

Natal Saturn conjunct the Solar Return MC indicates a time of professional responsibility; much may fall on your shoulders right now. It is a time of disciplined hard work and a lot can be achieved. If you are generally a hard-working type this can be a very rewarding time, when you are recognised for previous efforts. But if generally you avoid things that are demanding, this can feel a grim time, as there is no escape now and less reward.

Contacts to the Natal Chart Uranus from the Solar Return

When a planet in the Solar Return chart is contacting natal Uranus then that planet's principles are going to manifest in more of an event-orientated and externalised form during the coming year. Uranus is the planet of awakening, of surprise. It is unpredictable and brings events that can be exciting or disturbing, pleasing or alarming and probably all these things at different times.

With the Solar Return Moon contacting natal Uranus you would expect your emotional responses to be unpredictable and excitable. You will be behaving at your most idiosyncratic as you will want to express your uniqueness and differentness. You are likely to feel rather highly strung and alert, as if you were waiting for the next surprise to happen. It is a good time for taking emotional risks and for enjoying a changeable life-style. You might move home, or make domestic changes.

With the Solar Return Mercury contacting natal Uranus your thinking will be at its most original and inspired. You will be at your most mentally alert. You may develop new interests and your mind is open to unusual ideas and new perceptions. You may use gadgets or 'new technology' in some way, and if you have considered using a computer or word processor then now is the time to do it.

If the Solar Return Venus contacts natal Uranus you may find yourself wanting more freedom and independence in your relationship. You are susceptible to sudden infatuations and you will want excitement in your love-life.

You may want to feel freer of money and possessions too, and could get rid of things, and not want to be tied by financial commitments. It could also mean you earn money in an unusual way and collect unusual objects.

For artists this could be a particularly inspired and innovative time.

If natal Uranus is aspected by the Solar Return Mars you will have a strong desire for personal autonomy. You will be determined, undaunted, independent and freedom-orientated with an ability to act decisively. There is a need to release tension and an ability to take risks, to walk a tight-rope metaphorically.

With the Solar Return Jupiter in aspect to natal Uranus you will be at your most inventive regarding new schemes and future plans. This aspect is forward-thinking and your whole orientation will be towards the future and the possibilities it holds. Your mind is at its most adventurous and you may want to learn about something that stretches you. You will want to get to wherever you are headed for, and fast. You could be interested in foreign cultures, and you may want to travel to unusual places.

With the Solar Return Ascendant conjunct natal Uranus you will appear independent, and your need for freedom and autonomy will be visible. You will be expressing your individuality and uniqueness in how you meet the world. This could mean radical changes in your appearance, like unusual clothes or a new hairstyle, that underlines and demonstrates your differentness.

With the Solar Return IC conjunct natal Uranus you would expect changes in the home, possibly moving house, perhaps excitement and surprises around your home. It could also indicate deep security issues getting shaken up and unusual events and happenings in your most personal and private life.

If the Solar Return Descendant falls on natal Uranus then freedom within a relationship will be an issue. You may balk at any restrictions your partner attempts to impose and will easily feel trapped. You may simultaneously have fears of being abandoned, and anxieties about being rejected if you are dependent. This is a time to grapple with the whole issue of space and independence versus closeness and dependency in relationships and to reach some resolution within yourself.

On a more casual level, you may meet and make friends with new and unusual people with whom you would not ordinarily associate and who bring something different and exciting into your life.

If the Solar Return MC conjuncts natal Uranus then, within your career, something that allows you to be more your own person and to express your individuality usually occurs. If this is not possible because the existing conditions are rigidly restrictive then you may suddenly leave because the compromise you are making becomes intolerable to you, or you may act in such a way that you get fired. You want the independence and autonomy to operate as you decide at this time, so, it is a good time to take on more responsibilities.

Contacts to the Natal Chart Neptune from the Solar Return

A Neptunian influence on any planet in the Solar Return chart is always unworldly.

If it is the Solar Return Moon in aspect to natal Neptune then there is a yearning to merge and for there to be an at-oneness with others. There will be a sensitising of the feelings with a propensity to delude yourself, to be deceived or to be caught up in a fantasy. It is a time to be introspective, when the feeling nature is at its most open and there is a possibility of mystical or psychic experiences.

With a contact from natal Neptune to the Solar Return Mercury it is a time when your imagination will be particularly rich. You will have a finely tuned feeling understanding of people and situations, picking up on the subtler nuances of what is being shared and exchanged. It is a good time for all creative thinking and your mind is particularly intuitive and receptive. You will also be susceptible to confusion and liable to suffer from befuddled thinking. You could be forgetful and unable to focus or concentrate on what is in hand, because your mind is off somewhere else. This is particularly likely if you are not inspired by what you are supposed to be focusing on. You will need time to day-dream.

Solar Return Venus in aspect to natal Neptune indicates a longing for perfection and for the ideal in a love relationship. This brings with it the possibility of being disillusioned and dissapointed. You are open to being deceived or simply deceiving yourself and believing what you would like to believe. There is a tremendous yearning for romance.

For artists and those working in a creative medium this is a particularly inspirational time when your aesthetic sensitivity will be at its most highly refined. You will also be at your most 'tuned in' to what is artistically appealing to the public, so it could be a commercially successful time too.

With natal Neptune aspected by Solar Return Mars your energy will be diffused and there will be difficulty in focusing your energy in any one direction as you are aware of endless possibilities. It is therefore not a good time for attempting decisive action. There may be a lack of will-power and energy; you may simply need to sleep more. It is a good time to practise any of the martial arts, with their spiritual orientation.

You may feel confused and possibly guilty. Your personal boundaries, that is knowing what you will and will not do, are unclear. You are more open to sexual seductions and infidelities, and this could be at your initiative or with you playing a more passive role, but going along with things nevertheless. You could easily end up feeling disappointed.

Solar Return Jupiter in aspect to natal Neptune indicates a beneficial time from an abundance of sympathy and kindliness. Your receptivity to others is heightened and it is likely to be a time where care and helpfulness are both offered and received. There is a possibility of travel to exotic places, and of religious or spiritual pilgrimages.

With the Angles, Neptune will bring yearning for merging, an unworldly and possibly confused dimension to whichever Angle it conjuncts. The issues of the natal Neptune will be brought to bear on the area of life the Angle describes.

Natal Neptune conjunct the Solar Return Ascendant will be a year when you will be wearing rose-coloured spectacles and the world will look a nicer place. Some of the harsher realities of life will be too painful to confront with your enhanced sensitivity to suffering and as a result you may try various ways to escape from them. Simply not buying the newspapers might be your solution. You are prone to day-dreaming and others may see you as 'spaced out'. For you, your dreams are more important, and the glimpses you have of a higher order will be your inspiration.

With natal Neptune on the Solar Return IC, you will be longing for perfection within your most personal and private life. You want your home to have the atmosphere of a temple and you are particularly sensitive to any negative undercurrents. While you might find your dream home, don't bank on it: you may well find uncertainty and confusion around your home and domestic situation. It is a soul-searching time when you contemplate your psychic depths and your family heritage.

The Solar Return Descendant conjunct natal Neptune

indicates a year in which you will long for the ideal partner. This may mean you feel very dissatisfied with the one you have got, or, if you do not have a partner, that you fall in love with some unlikely person and imagine them to be ideal. However, you may find your ideal love, and at its highest this is a kind of spiritual love, where you are opened up to something divine. For many this will be a year where there is a lot of confusion within all relationships and friendships as you grapple to discover what the reality of the situation is.

If natal Neptune conjuncts the Solar Return MC then the whole focus of the year is rather ethereal, with your goals and achievements being of a higher, possibly spiritual kind. This can seem an extremely unproductive time as very little on a tangible level is achieved. You may easily see it as a waste of time and feel you are getting nowhere. You may wish to escape from the world. Some scandal, something you have kept hidden, may become known. It is a time to reappraise what in fact your goals are and to make sure they incorporate your higher ideals.

For artists and musicians and anyone working in film, the media, the fashion or glamour industries, then this could be a year in which some of your dreams become realised and you become known for your creativity.

Contacts to the Natal Chart Pluto from the Solar Return

Contacts to Pluto will draw a planet down to work less consciously and more compulsively and obsessively. The Solar Return planet's principles may also undergo deep psychological changes, changing its outer expression and way of manifesting.

If the Moon of the Solar Return falls on Pluto, memories buried deep within your unconscious are likely to surface during the year. Things will emerge that may have lain dormant for years. You might have some spontaneous cathartic releases with volcanic eruptions of emotion and buried feelings. These will bring with them a new understanding of yourself and what caused you to repress these feelings in the first place. You could also be reacting very strongly to things happening in your life now.

With Solar Return Mercury in aspect to natal Pluto you will be forceful in the way you express your ideas and opinions, possibly being a little overbearing. You are prone to be fanatical and to try to influence others. It is a good time for orators, for people involved in selling, and for politicians, as you have enhanced powers of persuasion.

Natal Pluto aspected by the Solar Return Venus indicates that you will have a charismatic attractive power and you may get involved in an intense love relationship. This may have an unfathomable and painful quality to it; it could be destructive in some way; it might have an obsessive or compulsive component. It is a time when deeper unconscious aspects of yourself are surfacing through a current relationship, through which you will come to understand yourself better. It could be that you are alone now, with no relationship, but still you will be focused on this lack and it will dominate your feelings.

If you are an artist your work may become more serious and profound. You may literally paint in darker colours, or metaphorically do so with other media of expression. Your work will be showing greater psychological depth and you may be preoccupied with matters of ultimate concern.

Solar Return Mars in aspect to natal Pluto indicates a year in which there will be an extraordinary working zeal with a determination to achieve a great deal. There is the capacity to work quite fanatically, to be ruthless and to succeed. You will be able to tap into and draw on inner resources of energy which sustain you through your endeavours.

More negatively, there is also the possibility of violence erupting. If this is something you have been on the end of, then it means you are having difficulties in expressing these principles constructively in your life. When Mars–Pluto energy implodes there can be feelings of hopelessness, powerlessness and despair, and a complete lack of energy resulting in lethargy and inertia. If this is how it is for you then you need help in releasing some of your depressed drive. Anything that gets your energy moving is helpful. There is usually fear of your own anger underlying these states.

With Jupiter in the Solar Return in aspect to natal Pluto it will be a year of extremes of some sort. It is a time of far-reaching endeavours and you will thrive on the risks you take. There is the possibility of becoming rich, either spiritually or materially. You may take your life to the brink of financial disaster and salvage things just in time, though there could be major losses too.

If the Angles of the Solar Return chart contact natal Pluto then you will expect to see some profound changes in the areas of life they describe.

With the Solar Return Ascendant conjunct natal Pluto then it will be a year when your intensity is very much to the fore. You will have powerful reactions to people and situations and are likely to set off powerful responses in others. This will be a year that signifies a major turning-point in your understanding of matters of ultimate concern to all people and will contain times of profound insight and awareness.

If the IC of the Solar Return chart conjuncts natal Pluto there will be complex issues within your most personal and private life. It is a time of deep psychological change. This might also manifest as changes to your home, particularly stripping down to the fabric of the building and rebuilding.

Natal Pluto conjunct the Solar Return Descendant indicates unfathomable things occurring in your relationships and friendships. This is the area of life where you feel most out of control, and where you will be trying hardest to exercise some control. Someone may come into your life who acts as a catalyst in some way, transforming your life, or you may act as a catalyst in someone else's life. You may find yourself in some kind of power struggle, which is ultimately teaching you about the effect you have on others and the reactions you draw to yourself that you are not aware of. The theme of the year is intensity in relationships.

With the Solar Return MC conjunct natal Pluto it is likely you will either be in or seeking a position of power. You will want to influence and change others and seek a position professionally that enables you to do this. You will have many ideas of how you would like to change the world in order to make it a better place. It is important you use your power and influence for these ends and not for your own personal ends as if you misuse power and are in any way corrupt this could be the year of your downfall.

Weighing up and Interpreting a Solar Return Chart

What we want to show you here is a sequence to follow in interpreting a Solar Return chart. With all interpretation you have to first take a chart apart and look at all its parts before putting the information you have gleaned back together in some kind of synthesised whole. If you try to synthesise too soon you loose both depth and detail in your understanding of the whole. Although the main themes in a chart will appear very quickly, it is important to examine everything in order to obtain a more intricate picture. While the list of factors that follows may seem arduous, it offers a reliable procedure which, it is hoped, will be particularly helpful to those who have not yet developed a personal technique of approaching the chart.

Once you have examined all the factors listed, the art of synthesis begins. You will generally find the main themes repeated in at least three different ways, each way giving more detail to the whole picture. The synthesis is in accurately interpreting these main themes. What follows is a list of factors to consider in building up a picture of the year ahead, in an order of importance in terms of giving both detailed and general information. The case studies in Chapters 9, 10 and 11 demonstrate further how to synthesise.

1.   The Sun's house position and aspects to the Sun within the Solar Return chart. This is the most important factor, as this tells you very immediately what area of life is most emphasised for the year. Refer to Chapters 1 and 2 for guidance on how to interpret these factors.

2.   The Ascendant and MC of the Solar Return chart. Any planets, both in the Solar Return chart and in the natal chart that conjunct the Ascendant and MC in the Solar Return. The sign, house position and aspects to the rulers of the Ascendant and the Midheaven. Chapter 3 and the earlier part of this chapter give guidance on interpreting these factors.

3.   The Moon, its sign, house position and the aspects to it within the Solar Return chart. The aspects the Solar Return Moon makes to the natal chart. Chapter 4 and the earlier part of this chapter gives guidance for the interpretation of these factors.

4.   The house emphasis, whether there are a majority of planets in angular, succedent or cadent houses. This will sometimes further emphasise the picture that emerged with the Angles, or it may contradict that picture and give a more balanced feel to the year.

With an angular house emphasis you would expect a year with a lot of activity, new projects beginning, new relationships commencing, and with you generally receiving a lot of attention. These are the action houses.

With a succedent house emphasis you would expect a year where your values were being strengthened; a year of responsibilities with character and maturity development. You may be stuck in a situation, or consolidating a past effort. This is a sustaining time.

With a cadent house emphasis you would expect a year of preparation, and of adaptation and training. Mental activity is emphasised, as are fluctuation and the consideration of alternatives.

The case studies in Chapter 9, 10 and 11 illustrate the different house emphasis.

5.   The main aspect patterns of the Solar Return chart. Look now too at any planets within the Solar Return not already considered. The first section in this chapter and the case studies in Chapter 9, 10 and 11 will help with these factors.

6.   Planets in aspect within the Solar Return chart that also form an aspect to each other within the natal chart. For example, if you have a Sun trine Saturn aspect in your Solar Return and a Sun–Saturn square in your natal chart, then this indicates a year when what has been an effort and a struggle becomes a pleasure and the motivation to achieve and succeed is experienced with ease. Conversely an easy aspect like a trine between planets in the natal chart, which can be something you take for granted about yourself and are lazy about and do not fully develop, can be spurred on to action in a year when they are in square in the Solar Return and latent talents can be realised. Whenever planets which are in aspect to each other in the natal chart are also in aspect in the Solar Return there is an opportunity to realise and develop something significant intrinsic to these planets' principles in terms of personal development. The case studies in Chapters 9, 10 and 11 will help with these factors.

7.   Planets in the Solar Return aspecting themselves in the natal chart.
   For example the Solar Return Moon trine natal Moon, which will give an ease, an at-homeness in the way you express your feelings and needs in the year. The Moon remains in a familiar element, you are at home in that mode. Solar Return Moon square natal Moon would be far less comfortable, for while the quadruplicity is familiar, there is more of a challenge to how you habitually are and a demand for you to respond differently. You are literally no longer in your element.
   Check at this point to see whether or not Mercury and Venus are in the same signs they are in natally. When in a different sign to the one they are in natally this will

indicate challenge and growth in their expression, and possibly more strain. If they are in the same sign as they are in natally, they are at home as it were and there will be an ease in their expression and therefore a lot of potential to maximise their principles.

The earlier section of this chapter will help in considering these factors.

8.   Aspects between the planets and Angles in the Solar Return chart and the planets and Angles in the natal chart – for example, the Solar Return Descendant conjunct natal Uranus. There is a section on interpreting these highly significant contacts earlier in this chapter.

6

HOW TO CALCULATE
SOLAR AND LUNAR RETURNS

We will be showing you a method of calculating Solar and Lunar Returns, using an ordinary calculator. If you are using a scientific calculator, which will divide and multiply in degrees and minutes, then the calculation is even simpler. For those of you who are anxious when dealing with numbers this is really very straightforward, and we have tried to explain the steps simply and clearly. For those who cannot face the calculation then most astrological computer software will do the job for you, if you have a computer, or you can send off to one of the computer services listed at the end of the book.

We do not make any adjustments for precession. We relocate the chart to the place where you are at the time of your Return. If you are away from home temporarily at the time of your Return you could use both the chart set for where you ordinarily are, plus the chart set for where you actually are, as they will both be of significance, but we would give most weight to the chart set for where you ordinarily are.

If you stay at the same location for over four years, you will notice that your Solar Returns are repeating a sequence, and that the house the Sun falls in follows a four-year pattern. This slowly shifts in a clockwise direction, so the pattern of houses occupied moves gradually over many years. This should be borne in mind as it has important implications in interpreting Solar Returns for someone who has stayed in the same place for over a decade (and when interpreting for businesses, organisations and countries).

All the calculation examples in this chapter are using Jack's chart, and they are interpreted in Chapter 9.

To Calculate a Solar Return

The Solar Return is a chart set up for the exact time that the Sun returns to the position it was at when you were born – that is, its natal position. This will happen some time close to your actual birthday, either the day before, the same day or the day after.

In order to calculate your Solar Return you have to calculate the time that this will occur. For those of you who are familiar with this technique (from calculating exact Ascendants), you are going to be carrying out a standard interpolation calculation. Once you have this, you simply set up a chart for this time, for the place you were at at that time.

The first thing you need to know, therefore, is the exact position in degrees, minutes and seconds, of your natal Sun. You need to know the seconds of the natal Sun's position in order to obtain an accurate Ascendant in the Solar Return chart. If your birth time is not accurate then your Solar Return chart will be inaccurate too.

Having ascertained the exact position of your natal Sun, to work out your Solar Return for any given year, find in the ephemeris the 24-hour period within which the Sun returns to its natal position, and proceed as follows.

Example

To find the time the Sun returns to its natal position of 29° 13' 20" ♎ in 1989. From *Raphael's Ephemeris* for 1989:

(1) Sun's longitude at noon on 23 October   0° 03' 31"

Sun's longitude at noon on 22 October   29° 03' 47"♏

Daily motion in 24 hours   59' 44"

Here we have established the daily motion of the Sun in the 24-hour period we are interested in.

(2) Sun's longitude at birth   29° 13' 20"♎

     Sun's longitude at noon on 22 October   29' 03' 47"♎

     Difference   9' 33"

Here we have established the difference in the Sun's position at noon to the natal position.

(3) We want to establish what the difference in position is in terms of time.

The standard equation to use for this is:

$$\text{Difference in time} = \frac{\text{Difference in mins. and secs.} \times 24}{\text{Daily motion}}$$

$$\text{Therefore difference in time} = \frac{24 \times 9' \, 33'' \text{ hours}}{59' \, 44''}$$

This is the standard equation we have to calculate in order to find the time of the Sun's return to its natal position.

If you have a scientific calculator you can proceed to calculate.

If you are using an ordinary calculator then it is necessary to change the seconds into decimals of minutes.

Table 6.1 is a conversion table. From this we can substitute:

$$9' \, 33'' = \frac{24 \times 9.55}{59.733}$$

Therefore 9' 33" = 3.837 hours.

Converting the decimals of an hour back into minutes

Conversion Table 6.1.   Minutes expressed as decimals of a degree or hour; seconds expressed as decimals of a minute

Mins./Secs.	Decimals	Mins./Secs.	Decimals
1	0.017	31	0.517
2	0.033	32	0.533
3	0.05	33	0.55
4	0.067	34	0.567
5	0.083	35	0.583
6	0.1	36	0.6
7	0.117	37	0.617
8	0.133	38	0.633
9	0.15	39	0.65
10	0.167	40	0.667
11	0.183	41	0.683
12	0.2	42	0.7
13	0.217	43	0.717
14	0.233	44	0.733
15	0.25	45	0.75
16	0.267	46	0.767
17	0.283	47	0.783
18	0.3	48	0.8
19	0.317	49	0.817
20	0.333	50	0.833
21	0.35	51	0.85
22	0.367	52	0.867
23	0.383	53	0.883
24	0.400	54	0.9
25	0.417	55	0.917
26	0.433	56	0.933
27	0.45	57	0.95
28	0.467	58	0.967
29	0.483	59	0.983
30	0.5	60	1

from the conversion table gives 3 hours and 50 minutes. This is the time after noon on 22 October. When calculating the Solar Return this is the interval.

Therefore the exact time of the Solar Return for 1989 is 3 50 p.m. GMT on 22 October.

In step 2 it is simplest to find the difference in motion that is shortest from either of the noon positions. So you could just as easily be subtracting the natal position from the later noon position. The important thing to remember here is that when you have converted the motion into the time equivalent (which is your interval) you subtract it from the later noon date, if you are using that, whereas in our example we used the earlier noon positions and so we added. It is just a matter of being consistent.

To set up Jack's Solar Return you proceed in the normal way. Jack was in Chelsea, London at the time of his Solar Return so the co-ordinates are 51 30 N and 0 7 W.

Solar Return date	22	10	89	
Latitude	51	30	N	
Longitude	0	7	W	
Time	H	M	S	
Solar Return time a.m.				
(GMT) p.m.	3	50		
Sidereal Time at noon	14	3	35	
Interval: to noon, a.m. −				
from noon, p.m. +	3	50		+
Result	17	53	35	
Acceleration on Interval:				
a.m. − p.m. +			35	+
Sidereal Time at				
Greenwich	17	54	10	
Longitude Equivalent:				
E + W −			28	−
Local Sidereal Time at				
Solar Return	17	53	42	

From tables of houses for 51 32 N the Ascendant is 25 degrees and 42 minutes of Pisces and the MC is 28 degrees and 30 minutes of Sagittarius.

Proceed to calculate the planetary positions in your usual way. The Interval of GMT is 3 hours and 50 minutes. The Log. of the Interval if using logarithm tables is 0.7966. The Calculator Constant if using a calculator is 3.833.

Jack's Solar Return with the planets' correct positions is shown in Chapter 9 in Figure 9.10. We are using Placidus houses. We draw in the natal positions in the outer wheel, in order to have a visual picture of the interaspects between the two charts.

To Calculate a Lunar Return

A Lunar Return is a chart set up for the exact time the Moon returns to its natal position. There are thirteen Lunar Returns in any twelve-month period. The procedure to calculate a Lunar Return is basically the same as the procedure to calculate a Solar Return.

Example

To find the Lunar Return that covers September 1990 for someone with their natal Moon at 10 degrees 13 minutes and 6 seconds of Pisces.

From *Raphael's Ephemeris* for 1990:

(1) Moon's longitude at noon on 5.9.90 is 18° 8' 26"
Moon's longitude at noon on 4.9.90 is 4° 26' 33"
Daily motion in 24 hours is   13° 41' 53"

This is the 24-hour period that we are interested in during which the Moon returns to its natal position, and we have established its motion.

(2) Moon's longitude at birth is   10° 13' 6"
    Moon's longitude at noon on 4.9.90 is 4° 26' 33"
    Difference is   5° 46' 33"

Here we have established the difference in the Moon's
position at noon to the natal position.

(3) We want to establish what the difference in position is in
terms of time. Note that from this stage positions rounded
up to the nearest minute will be accurate enough, as the
Moon is moving so much faster than the Sun.
   The standard equation to use for this is the same as that
on page 101.
Therefore difference in time = $\dfrac{24 \times 5° 47' \text{ hours}}{13° 42'}$

Use Table 6.1 to convert minutes into decimals of a degree,
thus:

$$5° 47' = \dfrac{24 \times 5.783 \text{ hours}}{13.7}$$
$$5° 47' = 10.13 \text{ hours}$$

Converting the decimals back into minutes from the
conversion table gives 10 hours 8 minutes. This is the
time after noon on 4.9.90, it is the interval from noon that
you use in calculating the Lunar Return, and gives the exact
time of the Lunar Return as 10.8 p.m. GMT.
   The chart is then erected in the usual way using the
latitude and longitude of the place the person was at at
that moment.

To Calculate Mercury, Venus and Mars Return Charts

To calculate Mercury, Venus and Mars Return charts the
procedure is identical to calculating Solar Returns. For
each of these you are setting up a chart for the exact time
Mercury, Venus or Mars returns to its natal position. So
with Mars you will have a new return chart approximately

every two years. And with Mercury and Venus rather more frequently, as they make their return to their natal position approximately once a year. As with the Sun, when calculating these return charts you need to have the natal position accurate to the nearest second, in order to calculate accurate Angles. For example, with Mars, if its natal position is only known in degrees and minutes, then at its return it will occupy this position for up to 40 minutes, which gives a huge variance on the Angles.

There are certain complications with these Return charts that you do not meet when calculating Solar and Lunar Returns. Mercury, Venus and Mars all have periods retrograde, and periods when they are stationary. While they are stationary or moving very slowly it is impossible to get accurate Angles and you have to use a chart that gives a much more limited picture. If they are moving at enough speed to give accurate Angles, but go retrograde around their return placement, then you will have three return charts to judge for that particular planet. It seems the final return before the planet moves off is the most significant for the time ahead. They are well worth pursuing despite these complications and if the calculation daunts you there is a computer service listed at the end of the book.

Timing Methods within Solar Returns

(1) Progressing the Moon

Take one day as representing the 12 months ahead. As the Moon moves between 12 and 15 degrees a day, this will give a motion of approximately 1 degree to 1 degree and 15 minutes a month.

For example, in Jack's Solar Return for 1989, shown in Chapter 9 in Figure 9.10, the Moon is at 12 degrees and 12 minutes of Leo. In order to progress the Moon first calculate its daily motion.

Moon's longitude at noon on 23.10.89 is   22° 43' ♌

Moon's longitude at noon on 22.10.89 is   10° 14' ♌
Difference is   12° 29'

This is the Moon's daily motion, which symbolises its motion for the twelve months ahead.

Divide 12° 29' by 12 and you obtain 1°2'25". This is the Moon's progressed motion per month.

To calculate the Moon's position for the 22nd of each month add 1 degree and 2 minutes, and 1 degree and 3 minutes, alternately, onto the position it holds in the Solar Return, as shown below.

Progressed Moon:

22.10.89	12° 12' ♌	22. 5.90	19° 29' ♌
22.11.89	13° 14' ♌	22. 6.90	20° 32' ♌
22.12.89	14° 17' ♌	22. 7.90	21° 34' ♌
22. 1.90	15° 19' ♌	22. 8.90	22° 37' ♌
22. 2.90	16° 22' ♌	22. 9.90	23° 39' ♌
22. 3.90	17° 24' ♌	22.10.90	24° 42' ♌
22. 4.90	18° 27' ♌		

When the progressed Solar Return Moon forms exact aspects within the Solar Return chart and makes exact aspects to natal planets this can be used to forecast events, turns of tide, trends in the year and inner change. We have found this to be particularly effective when setting off a tight aspect pattern within the Solar Return or natal chart.

(2) Transits

It may be worth using, in particular, the Sun's transits to the Solar Return, to forecast when issues indicated may come to prominence. We personally have not found this to be very effective, however.

(3) Progressing the Angles

The Angles are progressed by the Solar Arc. This is roughly 1 degree a day (365 days: 360 degrees).

To calculate exactly:

(a) To progress the MC to a given date:

Calculate the difference, in absolute longitude, of the Sun's position on the given date from the natal position. Add this on to the Solar Return MC. This is the progressed Solar Return MC.

(b) To progress the MC to any particular zodiac degree:

Substract absolute longitude of the Solar Return MC from the particular zodiac degree wanted. Add this to absolute longitude of Solar Return Sun. Convert this to zodiac position of Sun. Look up the date the Sun reaches this position in the ephemeris.

This is the date the progressed Solar Return MC reaches the particular degree.

An example of 3(a) follows.

Using Jack's Solar Return chart for 1989 shown in Chapter 9 in Figure 9.10.

To progress the MC to its position on 2.3.90, from *Raphael's Ephemeris*:

Sun's absolute longitude on 2.3.90	= 341° 39′
Sun's absolute longitude at birth	= 209° 13′
Difference is	132° 26′
Add this to the Solar Return MC absolute	
longitude of	268° 30′
Gives progressed Solar Return MC	400° 56′
Subtract	360°
Gives	40° 56′
in absolute longitude	= 10° 56′

This converts to 10° 56′ ♉

To work out the progressed Solar Return Ascendant, then look up the corresponding Ascendant in the tables of houses, using the correct latitude.

The progressed Solar Return Ascendant on 2.3.90, from tables of houses for 51°32′N is 23° 55′ ♌ .

An example of 3 (b) follows.
Still using Jack's chart, Figure 9.10.
To find out when the progressed MC will conjunct Jupiter.

Absolute longitude of Jupiter	100°	47'
Subtract absolute longitude of Solar Return MC	268°	30'
(Add 360 degrees to 100° 47' in order to do this)		
Difference	192°	17'
Add this to Sun's absolute longitude position	209°	13'
This gives	401°	30'
	41°	30'

Subtract 360 degrees in absolute longitude
This is 11° 30' ♉

Look up in the 1990 ephemeris the date the Sun reaches this zodiacal degree. It arrives at 11° 30' ♉ on 2 May 1990. Therefore the progressed Solar Return MC conjuncts Jupiter on 2 May 1990.

We find this an extremely useful timing technique. How to interpret these timing techniques in Jack's Solar Return chart is discussed in Chapter 9.

7

LUNAR RETURNS

A Lunar Return is a chart drawn up for the exact time the Moon returns to its natal position. This occurs, on average, every 27.32 days and is known as a sidereal month. There will be thirteen, or occasionally fourteen, Lunar Returns in any year.

Lunar Returns give a lunar picture of the month ahead; they show what will be of importance on a feeling level. They describe the mood and background tone of the month ahead. They tell you what life will be like on a day-to-day level. They tend to show the gentler ups and downs, rather than major events; the blips in life rather than the crises. The exception to this is when they reflect strongly and re-emphasise issues already described in either the natal chart or the Solar Return. When they underline a theme in this way, they then act as a timing technique and show that this is the month when this theme from the natal chart or the Solar Return will manifest most strongly.

When interpreting Lunar Returns there are certain key things to consider. The Angles of any chart provide the framework, in time and space, through which the planets' principles are expressed. It is important to relate the Angles to what the chart is describing. With Lunar Returns the MC indicates what you want on an emotional level; what your emotional ambitions are, and how you want to be seen in the context of your feeling side; how you want to project yourself.

The Ascendant will show how you seek to express your

emotional needs and how you approach getting your needs met. For example with an Aries MC you might be trying to get your own way, or wanting to be seen as someone who takes the lead. With a Libra MC you could want a relationship, or it could be important to you to be seen as fair. At any rate your aims of the month will be focused around Libran issues.

In a month with a Sagittarius MC your ambitions will be for personal freedom and independence. If at the same time the Moon was in the sixth house you could find yourself tied by practical considerations and balking against the restrictions; your aim is for freedom, but everyday reality demands your attention.

If the Ascendant were Sagittarius it would be a month when you feel you need the freedom to do exactly what you want when you want. If the Moon was in the sixth house then it could be a month when you are being challenged to come to grips with your freedom urges, through finding yourself feeling tied down by practicalities. You will want your freedom and autonomy very badly and feel stifled by the demands and restrictions that everyday life imposes.

The most important feature in a Lunar Return is the house position of the Moon. This will describe the area of life you are most preoccupied with on a day-to-day level in the month ahead. It will show where you look for emotional satisfaction, that is, what nurtures you and what you will be most emotionally involved in. There is a section that looks at the Moon through the twelve houses later in this chapter.

Angular planets in the Lunar Return chart are also highly significant. We allow orbs of about 5 degrees. Angular planets set the tone and flavour of the month. They will describe the current issue in a very immediate and obvious way. In some ways they will seem more important than the house position of the Moon, as this will be a subtler influence in a month with angular planets, lying beneath the surface of their more visible expression. When looking at a sequence of Lunar Returns for several months ahead, those with angular planets will be the months to pick out at a glance as being of particular significance, and especially so if the Sun or Moon are angular. A planet conjunct the Lunar Return MC will be describing the emotional aims of the month, while a planet conjunct the Ascendant will describe emotional needs. There is a section that looks in more detail at angular planets later in this chapter.

The house position of the Sun will also show an area of emphasis. Months with Sun–Moon aspects show an important time for progress or conflict, depending on the aspect, and involving the areas of life appropriate to their respective house positions. There will be periods of time when you have a sequence of Lunar Returns with varying aspects between the Sun and Moon. This will indicate a phase in your life where much can be achieved and resolved.

The aspect patterns within the Lunar Return will also be significant. Aspects to the Moon will be most significant, and show different principles that will be incorporated into your everyday life during the month indicated. As was said earlier, when aspect patterns within the Lunar Return reiterate themes shown in the natal chart or Solar Return then this will show the month when the issue indicated will manifest.

Finally, the interaspects between your natal chart and your Lunar Return are always significant, particularly when the Angles of the natal chart are involved. We are fairly flexible in the orbs we allow, but as a general rule we would suggest orbs of up to 2 or 3 degrees. Interaspects between your Lunar and Solar Return can also be significant, but tend to be less so, except when there are connections back to the natal chart as well, when they will be particularly important. The house in the Lunar Return that the ruler of your natal chart falls in also seems to be of more significance, and worth paying particular attention to. Its house seems to describe a second area of life where there will be an emphasis.

When interpreting Lunar Returns an understanding of

the condition of the Moon in the natal chart is crucial in building a picture of how the Moon operates in a person's life. Someone who has difficulty with the lunar principle, from difficult natal aspects to their Moon, is going to carry with them all the unresolved difficulties of their natal placement into their life in general. Each Lunar Return must then be interpreted with this constant inner difficulty in mind, and there will be pluses and minuses in the person's life accordingly.

In the interpretation of any chart, the main themes will be repeated and said in different ways several times, and the same is true in Lunar Returns. The main themes for the month will be signified more than once, so it is actually quite hard to miss them.

The following sections on the Moon through the houses and angular planets are intended to stimulate your thinking, and offer some possible interpretations. In Chapters 9, 10 and 11 we show far more complete interpretations of Lunar Returns, linked to the natal chart and other Return charts.

The Moon through The Houses

The Moon in the First House

With the Moon in the first you are likely to feel emotionally exposed and more vulnerable. You are more open to contact and may be actively seeking it. A lot will depend on how at ease you are with the lunar principle, how far you accept your own emotional needs, which the natal chart will describe. If you are relatively at peace within yourself, then this can be an open and receptive time, where the barriers between yourself and others come down. For others with more difficult natal Moons, then this degree of exposure can be excruciating, and indicate all too painfully how much conflict you have within yourself on a deeper level.

The Moon in the Second House

This is a month when issues around money and resources may predominate. The earning of money may be an emotional issue, and you may feel you need money or feel acutely a lack of it. You may be grappling with wider issues of your own resources, on both an inner and outer level. You may come up against a situation that forces you to be more aware of what inner reserves of emotional strength you have to draw on. You may be feeling the lack and extent to which you are without inner back-up. You could be concerned with security issues in general, what makes you feel emotionally secure, and what your inner qualities are that you can depend on for security.

The Moon in the Third House

This is a time when you will be involved with communication in some form. You will be making contact and connections through words, either spoken or written. This may be by writing letters, or articles, or disseminating information in some way. You may be talking to a lot of people, or involved in some local activity. A vivid example of a Lunar Return with the Moon in the third house is someone who was involved in canvassing and petitioning against a one-way system for traffic being implemented in their neighbourhood. It brought them into contact with a lot of local people, it attracted press coverage, and they gave out information locally, both written and through public meetings. More involvement in your local community is a distinct possibility during this month, though not necessarily nearly so active, possibly just on the level of noticing and minding about things going on more than usual.

Another possible scenario with this placement is a learning situation. You could be grappling in some way with something you are learning; either the subject itself could be emotionally involving you, or the learning situation might be stirring things up for you.

There might also be more involvement with a brother or sister. Something may arise with a sibling that absorbs your time and emotional energy. If ordinarily you do not have much to do with them then now is a good time to do so, or else to try to understand more about the distance between you and them.

The Moon in the Fourth House

Your inner most private and personal world will be the main focus for this month. This is likely to be an introspective time where your priorities will be to do with feeling settled and secure within yourself. This may be entirely on a feeling and psychological level, or it could be on an outer level with you being preoccupied with things to do with your home and family. Any changes occurring at this time within your home-life are likely to reflect emotional security needs. A sense of knowing where you belong will be heightened at this time. You will be looking for inner peace.

The Moon in the Fifth House

This is an extroverted month, and if life has been at all dull recently then it is likely to feel exciting and active in comparison. It is a month where entertainment will be strongly featured. You might simply socialise more, or go to a party, or to the theatre, or the ballet, or a concert. Whatever it is, any participation you have is likely to boost your energy and give you a renewed burst of vigour. Prior to this month you may have felt life was passing you by, and suddenly you are swept up by life and feel in the midst of things again. It could be someone else's authenticity that inspires you to feel and express your own creative energy, but however it happens you will feel revitalised and more completely yourself.

The Moon in the Sixth House

This is likely to be a month when you will be mainly concerned with your work, possibly your health, and the humdrum routines of everyday life. You may be working hard and finding great pleasure and emotional satisfaction from the work you are engaged in. You are deriving something from it that is important to you on an emotional level, in some way it is sustaining you. This could simply be from the money you are earning (particularly applicable to the self-employed), but it is likely to go deeper than that. There could also be emotional turmoil relating to work, depending on the aspects and the condition of your natal Moon.

You may also be involved in taking care of your health in lunar ways. One person with this placement in Cancer spent most of the month on a holiday visiting spas and saunas and becoming quite soporifically relaxed. Not everyone will have such a delightful time, but the question of physical and mental well-being, and how that relates to the balance in your life between things like your work, your diet, and whether you have sufficient exercise, fresh air, relaxation and sleep, may well arise.

The Moon in the Seventh House

This is a time when relationships are emphasised. If you are not in a close relationship then this will be a time when you are more likely to feel this as something lacking in your life. You could quite possibly make various efforts to find someone, by socialising more and generally putting yourself out. It is possible you will find an important new relationship, but it is quite likely you will not, and that you will end up in a more reconciled place within yourself regarding relationships. You may well end up knowing more about your own ambivalence and why you do not wish to be involved.

For those who are in a close relationship, then it is likely that a lot of your time and energy will be taken up with your relationship, and with how well it works for you. It could be a very pleasant time.

This is a month when you will be more open and responsive to friendship on all levels, not just the romantic. It is a time for examining the dynamics between you and others on all levels and of getting to know what you want and need and how satisfying this area of life is for you.

The Moon in the seventh house could also signify an important month with regard to contact with the public. Depending on the aspects, it is generally a favourable time for this as you are likely to be 'in tune' and to elicit a good response.

The Moon in the Eighth House

This will often be a very important month with regard to deep inner feelings, and can represent an emotional watershed. At the time it may not seem that significant or momentous, but with hindsight one can see that this month contained an important turning-point. This could be a turning-point in a friendship or relationship, usually leading towards greater intimacy. You may be more involved in relationship issues in a general way, and more prepared to examine things from a psychological perspective.

The Moon in the eighth could indicate a crisis (of any kind) that plunges you into deeper emotional states within yourself than you are generally familiar with. It could also be connected to money, with someone investing in you in some way.

The Moon in the Ninth House

The main focus of the month is likely to be around travel or study. You may be actually travelling this month, or emotionally involved in planning a journey. You may be involved in some form of study, which develops emotional complications (like falling in love with the tutor!). A more intimate situation may arise regarding study. You could also be involved yourself as a tutor or lecturer in some form of higher education, in which case you would have a high degree of emotional involvement. This could be with the subject you teach, or it could be you are preparing a lecture or writing an article that takes all your emotional energy.

One way or another, you are likely to go through a whole spectrum of emotional responses to some kind of ninth house stimuli, be it travel, study or teaching. In some way you will find greater emotional freedom and space this month; something emotionally liberating is likely to happen.

The Moon in the Tenth House

This is likely to be a time when your main emotional concerns will be to do with your professional status and standing in the world. It may be that you feel you have 'arrived' in some way, you are where you want to be and feeling pretty pleased about it. Or it may be that you are made abundantly aware that you are not where you would like to be. The month may contain a series of events that reflect your position. You are likely to be getting recognition in an area that matters to you and you may be doing some very concrete things that underline your achievements. You may do something yourself that promotes your work or asserts your importance, like giving a rather grand party. You want everyone to know and appreciate your position, and the degree of subtlety with which you do this will depend on your natal Moon's sign.

The Moon in the Eleventh House

This will be a month with the emphasis on your social life. You are likely to be socialising more than you usually do and emotionally involved in activities within your social circle. You may be assessing your place within your circle, and may want to strengthen your position within it in order to feel more secure. You want to feel you belong and are needed. This process may be going on in any groups, however loosely defined, of which you are a member. The extent to which you depend on the group or circle for your well-being will be accentuated. It could be a time when you feel the demands of the group are too high and you resist certain pressures and feel prepared to bow out if necessary. This could easily have the effect of strengthening your position.

For anyone working with groups or politically involved this should be a favourable month, depending on the Moon's aspects, as you will be particularly 'tuned in' to the group process and the public.

This could also indicate a time when you feel more connected to your ideals and beliefs in life in general and how they influence and serve your well-being.

The Moon in the Twelfth House

This is a time of retreat and withdrawal from the world. The world may seem a harsh place and you are likely to shrink from it and want to be alone to introspect and sift through your inner thoughts and feelings. This is a transition time, when you feel confused and have inner changes and decisions to make, but have not reached what they are yet; it's the rumblings of an inner change. You may recognise uncomfortable feelings within yourself and find yourself facing up to things you did not want to look at.

There may be complicated and confused things going on, particularly in your friendships with women. You could find them treacherous and manipulative. This is a reflection of your own current muddle and confusion and should recede as you emerge with greater clarity regarding your personal life.

This is a good time for going on an actual retreat, as this is the type of process you will be in anyway, or for meditation, contemplation and introspection within the framework of your ordinary life.

Angular Planets within the Lunar Return

What we will be looking at in this section is when a planet in the Lunar Return conjuncts one of the Angles of the Lunar Return. However, while we will not be going through other planet–Angle combinations, it is important to recognise that planets in the Lunar Return that conjunct the natal Angles are always significant; these will be transits to the natal chart, and the Lunar Return can give more detail in understanding these for that particular month. Also, natal planets conjuncting the Angles of the Lunar Return are always significant. The natal planet will be the background influence that will be channelled through a particular Angle.

The descriptions that follow are intended as prompts to get your own ideas flowing. Knowing how the various planetary principles operate within you and within your life will help enormously, as then you will begin to know what to expect. When interpreting someone else's chart, always start by looking at how the natal chart manifests and at the person's relationship to the different planetary principles. A Lunar Return must always be interpreted within this context.

The Sun Angular

The Sun on the Ascendant, Descendant or MC tends to mean you will be seen this month. One way or another you will be in the limelight.

With the Sun conjunct the Ascendant you are likely to be making an impact by way of your personality. You will be noticed by the people around you. You will approach getting your needs met with confidence. You will feel a need to be seen and will want recognition.

With the Sun on the IC you will be primarily involved with your inner and personal life. This is an introspective period, and may be a time to replenish from attending to your home and family and private world. You may receive certain recognition for playing an obscure role.

With the Sun conjunct the Descendant you will come across as confident and you may find yourself a 'star' in some way and receiving recognition. Depending on what you do ordinarily, you may well be in the limelight, making contact with others in a public way. It is a time when you will be noticed.

When the Sun is conjunct the MC you will command attention in some way as your main aim is to get yourself noticed. Depending on the scope for this within your life, you may be in the public eye and getting a certain amount of recognition.

The Moon Angular

The Moon angular is the most important planet to have angular in a Lunar Return. Some of the effects may be similar to the descriptions for the Sun, except with the Moon there will be more of an emotional involvement on your part with the events that take place.

With the Moon conjunct the Ascendant you will be particularly open to making contact with others, and sharing more of your private, inner feelings. You are likely to draw a genuine response from those you encounter, and to be making deeper contact. This could be painful, depending on how you feel about opening up to others. The earlier descriptions for the Moon in the first house also apply here.

With the Moon conjunct the IC you will be preoccupied with your home, family and inner personal life. It is likely to be a time of retreat from the outer world while you sort out certain inner and emotional priorities which will give you a secure basis within yourself from which to proceed. The whole question of where you belong and what home means may be reviewed at this time. The earlier descriptions for the Moon in the fourth house also apply here.

The Moon on the Descendant will emphasise all your personal relationships. You will be more sensitive to your own needs, and of how able you are to get them met. You will be both more receptive and more responsive to others throughout this month.

Any contact you have with the public is likely to be favourable, as you are likely to be well received. The earlier descriptions for the Moon in the seventh house also apply here.

If the Moon is conjunct the MC there is a coming together of your personal life with your ambitions and goals, and in some way you 'go public' this month. It could be that your emotional life and needs are your priority for this month and that you will put considerable energy and effort into your personal life. It is also likely that you will get a lot of public attention and recognition, which is important to you on an emotional level; it nurtures you. The earlier descriptions of the Moon in the tenth house also apply here.

Mercury Angular

Mercury angular in a Lunar Return emphasises communication of your needs.

With Mercury on the Ascendant you will simply be

talking a lot. It is likely to be within the domain of your ordinary life, and you will want to verbalise your needs and feelings more strongly than usual.

Mercury on the IC is a more introspective interest. You may be more curious about your past, or family lineage. You may be writing at home, or just mentally preoccupied with family and personal matters.

Mercury on the Descendant is likely to be about communications with others. Again you could be speaking publically, and what you have to say is really listened to. All one-to-one communication is also emphasised, and is likely to play an important part in the month.

With Mercury on the MC it is likely to be an important time for communication. This could be your giving voice to personal aims, or it could be communication in a public way that gives you recognition for your ideas and enhances your well-being.

Venus Angular

Venus angular in a Lunar Return is likely to increase your pursuit of pleasure and sociability for the month.

With Venus conjunct the Ascendant your approach to getting your needs met will be one of tact and diplomacy. You will be more concerned with your appearance and might get a new hairstyle or buy new clothes. You will also be more involved in relating and enjoy just being with people.

If Venus is on the IC you will be involved with your family and domestic situation. It could be an extremely enjoyable domestic time. You might be having a sociable time at home, with friends coming around, or giving a party. You might literally be decorating your home, although that is a bit energetic for Venus, and you are more likely to be lazing around at home being mildly debauched.

Venus conjunct the Descendant will probably be a very pleasant month on a social level. You are likely to be popular, and to receive invitations to do entertaining things with others. It could be important romantically, but it could just be a rather excessive and enjoyable time.

With Venus conjunct the MC it could be a time when charm, elegance and sociability help advance your career in some way. There may be social occasions where you need to put on a good appearance, and show you move in the right circles. This could be a very enjoyable time too, when you feel really pleased to be invited and included in social gatherings which in some way reflect your status. Alternatively, you might receive career help from a friend or lover at this time. It looks like a good time from a financial point of view, although you could also be rather extravagant.

Mars Angular

An angular Mars in a Lunar Return indicates a month with a lot of action and activity centred on lunar concerns. Things tend to happen with an angular Mars.

With Mars conjunct the Ascendant you will be more bombastic and forceful yourself, with a lot of energy for doing things and making demands for things you want. It could be a quite frenetic month.

Mars on the IC indicates that the action is going to be both home-based and psychological. It could be experienced as an emotionally frustrating time, with pent-up energy bursting forth. It is a good time for expressing old grievances. It could be the time to do the home decorating!

When Mars conjuncts the Descendant then the action involves others and your relating to them; it could be increased sexual activity, or competition, or rows, or energetic exchanges.

If Mars is on the MC you will be making an impact in the world. This is good for getting ahead where fierce competition and daring is called for. Alternatively, you might be putting a lot of energy into achieving personal ambitions, again taking big personal risks in order to realise what you want.

Jupiter Angular

Jupiter angular is optimistic, with a tendency towards being excessive. With this placement the danger is in hoping for too much. However, you will feel cheerful, even if all you expected does not materialise.

With Jupiter conjunct the Ascendant your approach to what you want is confident and happy-go-lucky. This tends to mean, because of your positive attitude, that you do in fact get what you want. However, even if things do not work out, you will bounce back this month, and nothing can seriously get you down. You are likely to break ground in some way in your interactions with others.

Jupiter on the IC will indicate a happy and expansive time at home on a personal and domestic level. It is a good time to have visitors staying in your home. It could also be a time to plan an extension! This could be literal, or represent a need in you for more psychological space and personal freedom. If you live in the country it is a good time for long hikes into surrounding areas.

If Jupiter is on the Descendant it will be a time when you have a greater faith in others and you may meet people who inspire you. It is a fortunate time for all your interactions with others; the only difficulty likely to arise will be if you expect too much.

With Jupiter on the MC you could well be feeling lucky in relation to your career or to goals you hold to do with your personal life. It is a good time for inspired moves on either of these fronts, and to trust your intuitions of what to do next. You will be aiming high and big right now and your optimism alone could take you a long way.

Saturn Angular

A strong Saturn tends to bring a serious time, where hard work, restrictions, and difficulties have to be faced. It could be a very productive time because of the amount of effort you are making, but it could also feel quite depressing.

With Saturn conjunct the Ascendant, then, your outlook and approach to what you need and want is serious and possibly pessimistic. Feeling pessimistic may actually be a more realistic outlook, and from this standpoint you may accomplish quite a lot, and feel satisfied by your achievements. You notice what needs doing and apply yourself to the tasks in hand. You need to work hard right now; you are in danger of worrying too much; you are at your most responsible.

When Saturn is on the IC you could feel rather lonely and withdrawn, or you might choose to spend time alone, finding it difficult to make satisfactory contact with others that is serious and profound enough for the frame of mind you are in right now.

Alternatively, on an outer level, you might be implementing concrete changes within your home. If this is the case, it may mean you encounter delays and obstacles in the process that test your endurance in some way.

Saturn conjunct the Descendant indicates a serious time for relationships. If you are in a relationship, then commitment issues are likely to arise; if you are not in one you may feel lonely. You are feeling at your least frivolous and want meaningful contact or none at all.

With Saturn on the MC then this is a month when you will take your aims seriously. This could well involve you in some hard work. You may realise some goal that gives you considerable emotional satisfaction. This goal could be a career goal that pleases you, or a personal goal that you apply yourself to achieving in a committed way.

Uranus Angular

With an Angular Uranus then expect the unexpected and the unpredictable. Within a Lunar Return the ups and downs of Uranus will probably not be that dramatic, as the influence is on an everyday and ordinary level. Nevertheless expect things on this level to hold upsets and surprises; Uranus brings what you are least expecting.

With Uranus on the Ascendant you are likely to be the surprising one in your life, so watch those impulses to behave in a wild way and think twice before getting your hair cut/dyed/permed or buying some outrageous and, by next month, unwearable clothes! You may well behave in ways you would normally consider shocking in an attempt to get what you want.

With Uranus on the IC there will be surprises within your home and personal life. Things will not go according to plan, and the more adaptable you can be the easier it will be for you.

Uranus on the Descendant can indicate a surprise of some sort in your relationships with others. Either you or they may want more freedom and independence. One of you may behave in an unpredictable way. Someone on whom you would like to be able to rely may seem unreliable. You might meet someone new who is unusual and outside of your ordinary circle of friends. Someone may shock you in some way. You may wake up to needs within yourself that you never knew you had.

With Uranus conjunct the MC there could be surprises, either with your career or with your goals within your personal life. You might act in a sudden way, or some opportunity may unexpectedly arise, or things around you could flair up in an unexpected way. It is a good time for you to get your own way. It is a time when you will refuse to make compromises.

Neptune Angular

Neptune conjunct one of the Angles can bring confusion and anxiety to that area of your life. A Neptune influence is always unworldly and can bring a longing for perfection.

With Neptune conjunct the Ascendant you will approach life and getting the things you want in an idealistic and potentially gullible way. You will tend to believe the best of everyone, and this may in fact bring out their better qualities, but you could also end up feeling disappointed and disillusioned. You will be prone to forgetfulness as your attention is likely to be on other faraway concerns. It is a good time for any unworldly activities.

Neptune on the IC is a time for day-dreaming at home. This is also an excellent time for meditation, contemplation and introspection. You may want your home to resemble a Buddhist temple right now, being a source of peace and stillness from which you can replenish yourself.

Conjunct the Descendant, Neptune could bring idealism, confusion, illusion, deception, or a yearning for perfection into your relationships with others. Any or several of these combinations might arise. You are particularly vulnerable to deceiving yourself regarding what is happening between you and someone else. However, it could be a truly magical month when things really are divine.

With Neptune on the MC your aims this month are for a kind of perfection. This could be a goal within your personal life that you long for particularly strongly right now, while contemplating how you might realise it. Or it could be you fantasising about an alternative career, and feeling dissatisfaction with the one you are in. You might be concerned with your spiritual goals, and where you feel you are as far as being on your true path in life.

Pluto Angular

Pluto is the planet of transformation, and the process usually hurts. Within a Lunar Return this is going to be a fairly minor transformation, unless the angular Pluto re-emphasises a theme from your natal chart.

With Pluto conjunct the Ascendant then it is you, your attitudes and your appearance that is changing. It could be an intense time, where you approach everything with a depth of feeling and a newfound intensity.

If Pluto is on the IC then your private domestic and personal life is being transformed. This is a psychologically profound time where incidents from the past might resurface to be reviewed. On an outer level it could indicate changes within your home, particularly the basement, and anything that involves stripping things down prior to any rebuilding.

Pluto conjunct the Descendant brings intensity to your contact with others. It is likely that you will be experiencing within yourself a greater depth of feeling, in response to someone else. This is a good time for a therapeutic exchange between you and another. It is a time when unfathomable occurrences with others are likely. If you are in touch with the public, you may now be able to mesmerise an audience. This could also extend into everyday contact.

With Pluto on the MC you could well be pursuing personal goals in a rather ruthless way. It might be a time when you feel you have no choice; it is a do or die type of situation. Or it could be a critical time in your career, where you are handed certain powers which you have to exercise. It is important to remain scrupulously ethical as any deviation on your part right now will certainly backfire on you.

8

MERCURY, VENUS
AND MARS RETURNS

Mercury, Venus and Mars Returns, like Solar and Lunar Returns, are charts drawn up for the moment the planet in question returns to its natal position. With Mercury and Venus this will be once a year while Mars will return once every two years.

These planets can, however, be retrograde or stationary and this can complicate the setting up of a return chart. It is possible for there to be three returns for a particular period if the planet retrogrades over its natal position. In this case it will be the last one that gives the picture of the time ahead and the others will tell about the intervals in between. In other words, a chart lasts for the duration of a return even if this is only for two weeks. Of course, it is possible that this could be a very significant two weeks in your life so it is wise to look at all the charts. If the planet is stationary then it will not be possible to calculate an accurate chart and in these circumstances it will be of limited value, although something can still be learned from the aspects to the return planet.

The information given by Mercury, Venus and Mars returns is an extremely detailed picture of the way that the planet in question is functioning during the period being looked at. They tell the story of the year, or years, ahead from the perspective of the planet concerned. The house position will show in what area of life you will be using that planet's energy – the kind of experiences and lessons that you will be involved in through its function. It shows what you have to learn at that particular time in order to develop the energy of the planet and use it in its most constructive way. The aspects will show what other energies have to be incorporated and how easy or difficult this will be to do.

In order to get a full picture it is important to work all round the chart as you would with a natal chart. Every detail will tell you something about how the planet is going to operate and how you can make the most of the opportunities and lessons it offers.

The angles of the return chart are going to be very important, especially if they are the same as your natal angles or if they fall on any planets in your natal chart. The Ascendant will show the way in which you express the energy of the return planet, how you go about using it at this particular time. The Midheaven will reveal what you are striving to achieve with this planet and how you will want the world to see you manifesting this planet's energy.

Angular planets in the return chart will be of great significance, giving further information about the qualities you will want to incorporate into the expression of the return planet. For example, the Moon on the MC in a Mars Return will show that you want to be seen as someone who acts responsively and caringly and your aims concerning the expression of Mars will be emotional ones. Your goal will be to take action that gets your emotional needs met.

If the return planet is conjunct the Sun, then this will be a very important period. You will be seeking to incorporate the energy of the return planet more fully into your identity and it will play a very important role in helping to define who you are. Through the expression of your return planet you will strengthen and develop your creative energy, giving you a more solid sense of your self and your purpose in life.

When looking at the other planets in a return chart it is important to bear in mind that in this chart they are functioning in relation to the return planet. So that, for instance, Venus in a Mercury Return will show how you seek to make loving contacts that stimulate your mind and enhance your communicative powers. Whereas, Mercury in a Venus Return will show your current state of thinking on love and relationships and how you will be communicating to those you love.

As you look at your return charts compare them with each other and to the Solar Return and look for any recurring themes. Important ones will show up in all the charts and often reflect unresolved issues from the natal chart. For example, if you have a difficult aspect between Venus and Pluto in your birth chart and all this year's return charts have a Venus – Pluto, Venus in the eighth or Venus in Scorpio theme, then this will be a time when you are drawn into something very deep which helps you to understand and resolve the difficulties of this powerfully transforming planetary energy.

Finally, always remember to refer back to the natal chart and especially to consider the condition of the return planet in question. The return chart will show how you go about developing the energy that you have and how your particular planetary pattern will be expressed. It will help you to understand the lessons to be learned and the ways in which you can work with the energy flow in order to develop its potential.

Mercury Returns

Before looking at the interpretation of Mercury Return charts it is helpful to consider the general principle of Mercury. Its function is one of linking and connecting and it represents the network which joins separate entities and brings them together. In the birth chart it shows our ability to communicate and make connections. Our ability to do this effectively defines how well or badly integrated we are with others.

It is the faculty by which we translate our imagery,

feelings and experiences into words so that we can share them with others. It is also how we process and digest the information that we receive. Mercury brings people together, making dialogue possible but it also emphasises their separateness and difference.

A Mercury return then shows how you process and digest what you learn in that particular year. It shows what your mind will be focused on and how you will approach the whole process of assimilating and disseminating knowledge.

The house that Mercury is in will show where your attention will be directed, what will interest you, what you will be thinking and talking about and what it is you have to learn, and how you will go about these things, during the period of this return. The aspects will show which other qualities you will try to incorporate and how easy or difficult you will find this, and will greatly affect your mental approach. The planets involved will indicate some of the main lessons to be learned during the year. For example, with Mercury conjunct Jupiter you will learn how to communicate more freely and openly and will be pushed to be more broad-minded and adventurous in your thinking. You will need to stretch and challenge your mind during this return. On the other hand, with Mercury conjunct Saturn, you will be learning to concentrate and discipline your mind. Your task will be to learn how to think and communicate in a more ordered and methodical way.

The Ascendant in a Mercury Return will show how you will want to express your ideas. In what way you will put yourself over to others and how you will connect with the world. If your return has Cancer rising, for instance, you will want to make an emotional contact with what you are interested in. You will need to feel strongly about subjects in order for them to interest you because you are looking for an emotional content in your mental activities. You will want to express yourself in a gentle and responsive way and may be reluctant to push your ideas forward.

The Mercury Return Midheaven is very important as it will show how you want to be seen as a communicator and how you go about achieving this.

It will show your current state of mind on what you want to achieve in life and where you are heading. For example, with Aries on the Midheaven, you will be thinking very clearly about what you want to achieve. You will want to put yourself over as an independent and decisive thinker. This will be a period when you are making plans and acting on them, a time of initiation and decision.

We will now look at Mercury through the houses.

Mercury in the First House

With Mercury in the first house, you are going to be very communicative. You will be learning about yourself and your world by talking, listening and making connections. You will be in the frame of mind to talk to everyone for you will understand that everyone has something to teach you. You will be interested in everybody and everything and will be insatiably curious.

Mercury in the Second House

During this return, your mind will be concentrated on practical issues and you are likely to be very resourceful about ideas for making money. Your mind will be full of plans for improving your finances and you will find the whole subject of money-making absorbing.

You will also be thinking about your real values and deciding what is really important to you, so that some of the values that have previously been important to you may be rethought now. You will be more flexible and open to new reasoning now.

This is a time when you are thinking in a very practical way and you will be concerned with ideas that you can put to good use rather than dreams and abstract concepts.

Mercury in the Third House

When Mercury is in the third house you are going to be somewhat mentally hyperactive. Your mind will be buzzing with ideas and you will have a great thirst for knowledge. It is a time for gathering information and developing your communication skills. This is a time of great activity and restlessness when you will want to be on the go all the time, moving around, talking to people and exchanging ideas. In your search for new interests, you may begin a new course of study that gives you a fresh framework for your ideas, so that you develop a new way of thinking.

Mercury in the Fourth House

A return with Mercury in the fourth house is likely to be a very significant time, especially if Mercury is conjunct the IC. You will be learning about yourself, journeying deep into the recesses of your feelings and memories. It is a time for reassessing and understanding your past experiences and for becoming aware of your deepest resources. You may discover and develop an innate talent at this time which helps you to develop confidence in your ideas. It is a good time for looking at your emotional needs more objectively and becoming aware of what you need in order to feel nourished.

Mercury in the Fifth House

This can be a very creative time when you need to give free rein to your imagination. You will enjoy playing with ideas and expressing them in a lively and imaginative way. You will be mentally stimulated by the arts and entertainment as other people's creativity will spark off your own train of thought. Your mind is likely to be more playful than usual and you will enjoy quizzes and games. You may also get a lot of pleasure from being with children as you feel more tuned in to their way of thinking and spontaneous self-expression.

Mercury in the Sixth House

With Mercury in the sixth house in your Mercury Return, you will be thinking a lot about work and making plans and decisions. You are likely to be doing a lot of mental work such as writing, teaching or planning work routines. It is a time for developing your ideas in a practical way and incorporating them into your everyday life. Matters connected with health and fitness are also likely to interest you and you may become involved in some sort of therapy or healing. You will be attracted to therapies that use the mind and imagination to heal people, such as guided imagery, or if your Mercury is in an earth sign you may find manipulative bodywork, such as massage, more appealing.

Mercury in the Seventh House

A Mercury Return with Mercury in the seventh house will see you in a frame of mind to share your ideas with those you are close to. It is a good time for sorting out differences in relationships as you will be more inclined to listen and discuss matters. You will feel a need to bounce your ideas off others and will be looking for feedback on your plans. This will be a very communicative time with a great deal of lively exchange and debate. You will find hearing someone else's ideas very stimulating and will get a lot of pleasure and satisfaction from working with others.

Mercury in the Eighth House

With Mercury in the eighth house you are likely to experience a time of intense thought and obsessive interests. You will want to probe other people's innermost thoughts and communicate on a very intimate level. Anything superficial will bore you stiff at the moment and you may find your mind dwelling on sex and death as you search for understanding of some of life's mysteries. This can be a time of transformation in your thinking as the depth of your mental involvement causes you to cast off old ideas, allowing fresh ones to rise from deep inside.

Mercury in the Ninth House

When Mercury is in the ninth house, you are going to be preoccupied with seeking knowledge and wisdom. You will want to understand more about the universe and how things fit together. There will be a feeling of restlessness as your thoughts turn to travel and faraway places. You may begin to study a subject that really opens up your mind to new concepts. You will be eager to discuss your views with others and to hear as many different points of view as possible. This can be a time of long philosophical conversations deep into the night.

Mercury in the Tenth House

At a time when Mercury is in the tenth house, your thoughts are going to be concentrated on your career and long-term aims. You may begin a new job which involves creative writing, public speaking, selling or trading. You will have lots of ideas about what you want to do in life and may start several new lines of work at once. Success may bring about a change in the way you think about yourself.

You will be thinking about improving your career prospects and may begin a course that is directly related to this, perhaps to gain a professional qualification. This is an excellent time for 'selling' yourself in the outer world as you are able to express your ideas in such a way that they impress others and bring recognition.

Mercury in the Eleventh House

With Mercury in the eleventh house, you are going to be re-evaluating your dreams and aspirations. Have you been heading where you want to go? Or have you lost sight of your dreams? This is a time when you will be thinking about where you truly want to go and may well find a new direction in life. You have a vision about how you want the future to be and set about planning its fulfilment.

During this period you need friends and groups who stimulate your mind and who share your ideas and ideals. It is important for you to be able to talk about your hopes and plans for the future and to be with others who foster and encourage you. It is also a good time for working on group projects or as part of a team.

Mercury in the Twelfth House

During a return with Mercury in the twelfth house you are going to experience a feeling of wanting to withdraw from communication. You will want to be on your own as much as possible in order to sort out your thoughts. It is a time of inward journeying and soul-searching. Memories, feelings and thoughts rise to the surface as you sift through them. It is a period for dreaming, musing and meditation and you will want plenty of time to ponder your own thoughts. This would be a good time to start keeping a dream journal as you will learn a lot about yourself by doing this. At this time you can be very creative mentally if you allow your mind to wander and play with your ideas. Solutions to problems are likely to pop into your mind when you are least expecting them.

Venus Returns

Venus in the birth chart shows how we seek to make loving contacts with others in order to become more whole. It shows how and what we love, what we look for to make us happy, the things and people we value and what we find beautiful – our aesthetic sense. Venus defines what we need from others in order to feel loved and the way in which we express our love.

The Venus Return then shows how you will approach love and other relationships during that particular time. It shows what you are looking for from relationships and the sort of people you will be drawn to. It will show what will make you happy and how easily this will be achieved.

As in all return charts, the house containing the return planet will be the most significant factor. In this case then, the house position of Venus will show what you are looking for in love and what sort of relationships you are seeking to establish and the area of life where you seek happiness.

The aspects to Venus will show the way in which this happens and will colour your choices and the way you go about finding love and happiness. So that, for example, if Venus is in the fifth house, but forming a square to Saturn, then although fun and pleasure will be the avenue through which you seek love, the aspect to Saturn means that it may be a struggle to find. It can also indicate that when you do find it, it may be a rather more serious or burdensome relationship than you had wanted.

If Venus is unaspected then it may be difficult to bring love into your life and you may feel somewhat cut off and lonely. It will be hard for you to make close connections.

The Ascendant in a Venus Return will show the way in which you seek self-expression through love. If the Ascendant falls on a natal planet then this planet's energy is going to be very significant in the way you relate and you will be developing the natal potential of this planet through your relationships this year.

The Venus Return Midheaven shows your conscious aims concerning the Venus principle. It reveals how you wish to be seen in relationships at this time and can also be a pointer to the kind of people who, through their relationship to you, will help to foster your career interests.

Angles which are the same as your natal ones are always significant and will indicate a crucial time in the growth of your ability to love and forge relationships.

We will now look at Venus through the houses.

Venus in the First House

A Venus Return with Venus in the first house indicates a time when there are going to be some very important lessons to be learned about how you relate to the world. Relationships are going to be at the forefront of your attention during this period and you will face challenges to develop your skills of interaction. A love relationship may cause you to see yourself in a different light and will colour the way in which you look at life. This is a time when you are learning to be yourself in the company of others and discovering how to maintain your individuality, while increasing the quality and intimacy of your connections with others.

Venus in the Second House

With Venus in the second, you are going to be concerned with the material and physical side of life. You will enjoy spending money on things that you value and which truly reflect your taste. It is a time when you are likely to find it easier to earn more money as it seems to flow in more easily than usual. But you are also likely to feel much more self-indulgent and extravagant than you normally are, so that you may be inclined to spend a lot more too. This is a time for getting the balance right, while at the same time being generous to yourself and giving yourself what you need.

Venus in the Third House

When Venus is in the third house you are going to enjoy conversation, socialising, reading and learning, so you may well make new friends or meet lovers through evening classes or some other educational activity! You will feel the need to share your ideas and will be attracted to lively, communicative people. This is quite a restless time with lots of different social activities. There will be a strong need to communicate with your loved one and you may find yourself conducting a relationship through love letters and phone-calls!

Venus in the Fourth House

This is likely to be a quiet time, when you enjoy being at home with your family and with others that you feel comfortable with. You feel the need to get really close to people so that existing relationships may deepen and become more intimate now. Relationships are likely to stir up memories from your early life, making this a particularly good time for therapy.

Venus in the Fifth House

This is a period when you will tend to be in love with love and you long to meet someone special. You will want to enjoy yourself and will get great pleasure from artistic and cultural activities, especially if you can share them with a loved one. You are likely to meet new friends and lovers through entertainment, creative pastimes or sport. It is a time for giving yourself a good time, for having fun, playing and generally enjoying life.

Venus in the Sixth House

With Venus in the sixth, your social life is likely to revolve around your work. You enjoy working with people and may even fall in love with a workmate. Friendships blossom at work and you may develop a working partnership which gives you great pleasure.

You are also likely to get a lot of pleasure from taking care of yourself and others. This is a time when eating a healthy diet and going to exercise classes will seem more like pleasure than duty. The physical side of love, too, is likely to become much more important and this can have a very beneficial and healing effect on your relationship with your body.

Venus in the Seventh House

With Venus in the Seventh House there will be a tremendous emphasis on relationships, which will become an issue that has to be sorted out. If you are not in a close relationship then you are likely to become aware of your need to love and be loved. If you are already involved with someone, you will now become aware of the ways in which this relationship falls short of your expectations. You will be wanting the perfect relationship at this time and nothing less will seem good enough to you. You may end a relationship which no longer meets your needs or you may begin a new one. You are seeking happiness through other people at the moment and will want to feel in perfect harmony with the person you love.

Venus in the Eighth House

A return with Venus in the eighth house indicates a time when you are seeking total transformation through love.

You want to be taken to the very depths of yourself and to touch souls with someone else. Love may be very painful at the moment and you may even develop an obsession with someone who does not want to know. But even if it is traumatic you will feel more alive because of the intensity of your love. Sexual desire and passion are very important to you now and you will be looking for this in your relationships. You will not be satisfied with anything casual or superficial but will want to take love to the limit.

Venus in the Ninth House

This is a time of restless searching for someone outside your normal sphere. You are looking for people who can enhance your understanding and give you a new perspective on the world. You are likely to be attracted to those who are very different from you in some way, perhaps coming from a different culture or social group.

You will enjoy studying at this time and are likely to meet new people this way. Or you could fall in love with a teacher, especially one from another country!

During the period of this return, you will be seeking a meeting of minds rather than physical intimacy and are going to feel a much greater need for space and freedom than usual.

Venus in the Tenth House

With Venus in the tenth house, relationships tend to be focused around your career and what you want to achieve in life. You are likely to cultivate the right people in order to get on in your work and will be attracted to those who are successful and who can help you. Career matters go well for you and you may actually achieve something you have been aiming for and wanting for a long time. Success will bring great personal happiness to you now and will help to heal any wounds in your self-esteem. You will learn to love yourself more through your achievements.

Venus in the Eleventh House

When Venus is in the eleventh house, friendship is going to be of paramount importance to you and you are really going to enjoy being with groups of people. You may join idealistic or self-improvement groups as you will want to be with like-minded people who share your aspirations. It is through group activities that you make friends and meet potential lovers, as shared ideals will be the basis of any new relationship at this time.

Venus in the Twelfth House

A return with Venus in the twelfth house is likely to be a time when you feel more withdrawn than usual and tend to relate to people in your imagination rather than in reality. You may dream of a perfect lover and find it hard to settle for anything less or you may just feel happier dwelling in your dream world. This is a time when helping others brings happiness as there is a selfless urge to serve which brings great satisfaction. You may also be called upon to make sacrifices for your loved ones and this, too, will bring inner peace as other people's happiness means more to you than your own at this time.

Mars Returns

Before beginning to interpret Mars Return charts we need to remind ourselves of exactly what Mars symbolises in the natal chart. It is essentially the principle by which we seek to assert our individuality. It shows the way in which we act in order to meet the Sun's needs. Mars is how we fight for survival as an individual in order to preserve our separate identity and resist the pressures put upon us to conform and compromise. It is how we express our energy and how we act; the way in which we actually do things. Mars also shows what, and who, we want and desire and how we go about getting these needs met. So that, for example, someone with Mars in Taurus will want stability, security and will need to build something solid and real and they will act in a methodical, thorough way in order to achieve this. Whereas, conversely, someone with Mars in Sagittarius will want space and freedom of movement and will act impulsively, spontaneously and enthusiastically.

A Mars Return, then, will tell you how you will use your energy to go about getting what you want over its two-year period. It shows what you most need to do in order to feel vital and alive and how you can act most effectively. It will also show the kind of people you are likely to be sexually attracted to at this time. This will be directly related to what you most need to develop your Mars energy. These people will have something to teach you about how successfully, or otherwise, you are using Mars.

Generally speaking, a Mars Return can be interpreted in much the same way as a Solar Return except that you need to bear in mind that it is telling you how you act and direct your energy. Because Mars symbolises action and doing, a Mars Return tends to be very clear and concrete. It is quite straightforward and direct compared with the subtler influences of Venus and Lunar Returns and this makes it simpler to interpret.

The house that Mars is in will show the main focus of your energy, where you need to take action and what you most want to do – what it is that will stimulate your energy most. It shows where you have to fight for what you want and the field of battle at that particular time. It is the area of life where you may be forced to fight for survival as an individual. The house of Mars tells where you can most effectively direct your energy and what you need to do in order to feel most alive. If you feel that you are not fully in touch with your Mars energy, then it would be helpful to make a conscious effort to concentrate your energy on the affairs of the house that Mars is in. This will stimulate the Mars principle and help you to get more in touch with it.

The aspects to Mars will show the qualities that you need to incorporate into the functioning of Mars at this time. For instance, if you have a Mars–Uranus aspect, you will need to develop your independence of action and are likely to be attracted to Uranian people and situations which help you to do this. The type of aspect will show whether this will be a smooth transition or a struggle.

The Ascending sign in a Mars Return will show the way in which you actually express your Mars energy during its duration. It will also indicate how you act in new situations, in what way you meet challenges at that particular time and the way in which you initiate new courses of action. For example, with Sagittarius rising, you will be full of enthusiasm and daring – leaping to meet challenges and taking everything on with optimism and enthusiasm. You will feel most alive when you are doing what you enjoy and may express your energy through sport, travel or study. It will be vital for you to have plenty of freedom of movement and to be physically active. In contrast, with Scorpio rising, your energy will be much more intense and inwardly directed and you may put a great deal of energy into self-transformation. You will need total involvement in what you do and will want it to have a profound effect on you. Your energy will be very concentrated at this time and you won't waste it on anything superficial. It can be a period of working obsessively on one particular project.

The Midheaven in a Mars Return reveals your aims for the period – what you want to achieve by your actions and how you go about achieving it. It also shows the image you wish to project to the world through the Mars principle. With Libra on the Midheaven, for example, your aim may well be to get into a relationship but you may find it hard to know exactly how to go about it. Libra is too concerned with its relationship to others to combine comfortably with Mars. It will be difficult for you to be direct about what you want as you will be trying to project an image of someone who acts very reasonably and rationally, so you will tend to be very diplomatic in your actions. On the other hand with Leo on the Midheaven, you will want to make your mark as an individual and will put your energy into achieving that with vigour and directness. You will know exactly what you want to do and how to get it and will want to project an image of dignified and authoritative action.

If the Angles of your Mars Return are the same as in your natal chart then this will be an extremely significant period for you during which Mars will be instrumental in developing the potential of the natal angles.

A return with Mars on one of the angles will also be a very important time for you but now it will be the development of your Mars energy itself that will be very much emphasised. How this is likely to manifest is shown by the interpretation of Mars in the angular houses in the section that follows.

We will now look at Mars through the houses.

Mars in the First House

With Mars in the first house you are going to be meeting life head on. You will want to test yourself against the world and will set up lots of challenges for yourself in order to discover the full potency of your Mars energy. This could be a period of battles and conflicts as you test your growing independence and strength. You will be learning to assert yourself and to identify exactly what it is you need from life in order to be yourself. It is a time when you need to take charge of your own life and go all out for what you want.

Mars in the Second House

Mars in the second house indicates a period when you direct your energy towards getting the things you really want. You take action to build something solid and lasting for yourself, something that you truly value. Money and material matters are a big issue for you at this time and you will fight hard to get them and to hold on to them. You are likely to be feeling much more acquisitive and possessive than usual at the moment because you are defining yourself through what you have. Therefore, your possessions are of vital importance to you as you are using them as a yardstick to your own value. You will really attack the business of earning money and work tirelessly to acquire the things you need in order to feel secure and worthwhile.

Mars in the Third House

A Mars Return with Mars in the third house will be a time of great activity, both physical and mental. You will feel very restless and may find it hard to concentrate on anything for long. You need lots of different activities and you may start several new undertakings at once. You will feel an urgency to acquire as much information as possible and will throw yourself with vigour into studying, writing and communicating your ideas. Everything seems to interest you and the more you learn, the more energetic you become. You need mental stimulation in order to feel alive at this time. You may also become more argumentative than usual and find yourself embroiled in hotly defending your ideas.

Mars in the Fourth House

When Mars is in the fourth house your energy is going to be focused on your home, which may become an emotional minefield. There may be a threat to your home and security so that you feel as though the ground is being cut from under you. Home is likely to be a battleground and you may be subject to a lot of emotional blackmail and manipulation. It can, however, be a very therapeutic time as a great deal of buried anger and passion is brought to the surface and you are likely to discover hidden reserves of energy and strength through working with difficult issues.

Mars in the Fifth House

Mars in the fifth indicates a period when you are revitalised by doing the things you enjoy. This is a time when you use your energy for pleasure and you are able to attack creative activities with a new dynamism. If you have ever thought of learning to paint, joining a drama group or taking up a sport, then this is the time to do it. You will also get immense pleasure from competition, so sporting activities are particularly invigorating right now.

You may put a lot of energy into love affairs and could be strongly attracted to someone you meet through a shared pleasure. Sex becomes a means of self-expression to you and you are likely to seek out new experiences.

Doing what gives you pleasure and having fun will be the way that you are learning to define yourself and what you want at the moment – so go ahead and enjoy it!

Mars in the Sixth House

With Mars in the sixth house, this is likely to be a period of very hard work. You may have decisions to make about your working life or have to replan your working routines. There is the possibility of quite a lot of conflict and disagreement with co-workers as unresolved issues are forced to the surface.

Your health, too, is likely to become a matter of concern to you. If your energy is low, you will notice it at this time and will want to do something about it. Illness may be caused by the suppression of anger and this is a good time for therapies which help with its release. It is also a good time for taking an assertiveness training course which will help you to learn to use your Mars energy in a more constructive way. You are likely to take steps to increase your general level of fitness, working out healthier routines and taking up exercise which improves your physical health and well-being.

Mars in the Seventh House

Close relationships may be something of a battlefield for you in a period with Mars in the seventh house. You are attempting to define yourself through your relationships to others and at times may feel that your freedom of action is threatened. In reaction you are likely to strike out and become angry with others in order to emphasise your difference and separateness. This can make intimate partnerships quite tempestuous, to say the least! This could be a time when you decide to leave a relationship that is not giving you what you want or from which the sexual attraction has died.

There will be a tendency to see others as opposed to you and to throw yourself into battle as you fight for the right to be yourself.

You will be putting a lot of energy into your relationships at the moment, which makes them very dynamic, so that you feel invigorated and refreshed by them. This can signify the beginning of a new relationship with someone you are very strongly attracted to and who you feel very stimulated by.

Mars in the Eighth House

During a year with Mars in the eighth house, you are going to be somewhat obsessive about what you do. You will want things passionately and will work intensely hard to get them, pushing yourself to the limits at times. This is going to be a time of transformation in the way you use your Mars energy and this will be brought about through the depth and intensity of your experiences.

Your sexual desires are likely to be intensified at the moment and you may become involved in a compulsive affair which releases hidden passions. It is a time of sexual discovery so that existing relationships can take on a new depth and excitement.

As with all eighth house placements, this can also be a traumatic time when something very painful happens. This could be the break-up of an intimate relationship, the death of someone close, or financial hardship, or it could be a time of dark depression and bleak despair. But whether the suffering is coming from inside or caused by an outer event, you will be called upon to dig into your deepest reserves of energy and courage and from this you will develop new depths of strength and power.

Mars in the Ninth House

Mars in the ninth house shows a time of widening horizons as you take action to open up your life. If you have ever dreamed of dropping everything and setting off round the world, then this is the time when you may actually do it. Even if you do not take quite such a drastic step, you will be wanting to move around a lot at the moment so travel is likely to be high on your agenda.

It is a period when you may become actively involved in studying philosophy or other subjects that challenge you and expand your knowledge. Being with fellow students will be stimulating to you and discussing what you have learnt will make you feel more alive. You may also find yourself fighting to defend your ideas and philosophical ideals as an attack on them can seem like a threat to your very survival.

You are likely to feel very restless at this time and you may tend to rush from one thing to another in rather a frenetic way as you search for stimulating and meaningful activities. You will want to do things that challenge you, both physically and mentally and will feel refreshed by doing things that are difficult, even perhaps dangerous. So it is a time when you may take up an activity that really challenges you, like mountaineering, flying or parachuting. Even if the things that you do are not physically dangerous, you will want to take risks in your life and do things that are personally challenging in order to free up your Mars energy.

Mars in the Tenth House

With Mars in the tenth house you will be taking action to secure your long-term aims. So it is a time when you may leave a job in order to start a new, more stimulating career. You will want to be fully engaged in your work at the moment and will become frustrated with boring or unimportant chores. Setbacks and upsets in your career will trigger off unconscious anger as you are reminded of earlier conflicts with parents and other authority-figures but these difficulties will stimulate your energy and make you even more determined to succeed.

This is a period when you feel extremely ambitious and will want to concentrate all you energy on your career and success in the world. You are likely to feel very competitive and your will to succeed will be very strong. Achieving your aims seems like a matter of life and death at this time, which can lead to conflict with those you perceive as standing in your way or with people who are in competition for what you want.

Mars in the Eleventh House

During a Mars Return with Mars in the eleventh, you are likely to take action to bring about the fulfilment of your dearest wishes. It is a time for making your aspirations and hopes for the future a reality. You are also likely to put a lot of energy into group activities and friendship. Because of the increased intensity there may be quarrels with friends at this time and some friendships may end.

You will find that you are energised by working together with others at the moment, so it is a good time for working on group projects. You will be able to accomplish much more by co-operating with others now than by working on your own.

Mars in the Twelfth House

When the Mars Return has Mars in the twelfth house, it is likely to be a period of reflection and inner development. You are going to be less outgoing than usual and less concerned with material matters. It is a time for digging down into hidden emotions and you may find that a lot of buried anger rises to the surface, especially in your dreams. You may put a lot of energy into exploring the mystical and spiritual side of your nature and may feel attracted to working in a selfless way to help others, perhaps in a hospital or other institution.

This can be quite a difficult time as the twelfth house is concerned with the surrender of self which is directly opposed to the Mars principle. So you will be learning to set aside your own personal desires in order to act for the benefit of others. This is a time for letting go of fixed desires and learning to go with the flow of life.

9

DETAILED CASE STUDY

The first case study we want to present is for Jack. Jack was in therapy with Babs for seventeen months, from August 1983 to January 1985 and since then has seen her once or twice a year for an astrological consultation. In presenting this study we have the advantage of an intimate knowledge of how he has used his potential and dealt with his difficulties to date – that is, how his birth chart has manifested.

We will be looking at his Solar Return for 1988 to 1989 in detail and briefly at a sequence of four Lunar Returns for this period. We will then look at his Solar Return for 1989 to 1990, and his Mercury Return for this period. Mercury is the ruler of both the Ascendant and MC of his natal chart and its principle is therefore more important and crucial in Jack's life than Venus or Mars.

We want to start, however, by going over Jack's natal chart, shown in Figure 9.1, and personal history in some detail, as this is something we have and can build our later interpretations upon.

When Jack began therapy, Pluto had transited his Venus and was now heading for the second transit of his Sun. Uranus had already opposed his Mars and squared his Pluto and was about to square his Moon, setting off his T-square. This certainly looked like an important time, a time of deep and profound change.

Just before he had arrived for therapy he had been involved in a fight in which his front teeth had been

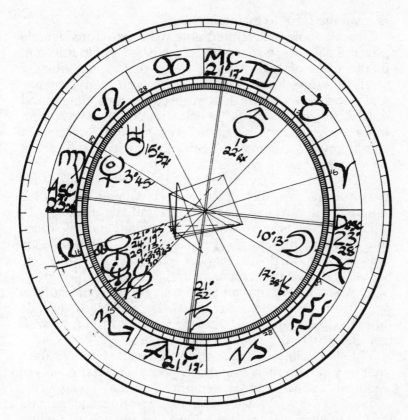

Fig. 9.1. Jack's natal chart (data witheld)

broken. He had a temporary bridge. He planned to sue the man who had done this to him for the money to pay for the treatment of a permanent bridge to replace his broken teeth.

It seemed very significant that with a Pluto transit to a Venus and Sun in Libra in the second house issues around his looks, his appearance were coming up. Someone from outside, Pluto, had come and attempted to destroy them, but he was intent on hanging on to them. He valued them (second house) extremely highly. The cosmetic bridge he had made cost well over £1000 and he ended up paying for it himself. The value he placed on his looks was high and he paid the price to maintain them.

This all took many months and he had considerable physical pain associated with this. He had a mild infection in the roots of one of these teeth, that would literally swell up when he was not in touch with angry feelings and subside when he had realised he was angry and did whatever it was he needed to do. It was like an inner barometer of when he was making too great a compromise, a Libran and Venus propensity that he could no longer get away with.

Let us take an overview of Jack's chart. He is an air/water person, sensitive, feeling and perceptive and with all his mutability he was extremely flexible and adaptable.

His Mercury is very strong as Ascendant and MC ruler, and conjunct Jupiter in Scorpio he was an opportunist. He was quick to grasp whatever came his way. He was quick-witted and versatile, optimistic and easy-going. Moreover, with Mercury, an amoral planet, in the sign of Scorpio, which can be positively criminal, he had his own code of behaviour, which was not necessarily in accord with society's; there is no Saturn contact here.

With his stellium, including his chart ruler in the second, money was extremely important to him. He wanted lots of money to spend in a free, generous and easy-going way.

He was very talented creatively, painting and singing and playing music. He presented two main issues when he began therapy with me. To date he had been exclusively homosexual; he had never related sexually to a woman. But now for the first time he was having fantasies of being with a woman, and also of fathering a child.

He also used cocaine on a daily basis and wanted to stop. He was very psychologically dependent on it. His whole life revolved around it. All his friendships were based on taking cocaine together. It was going to involve a massive change for him to stop as it was central to his life. All his friends ever seemed to do was visit each other with their supply of cocaine and take it together. No one would visit him anymore if he stopped, and he could not visit anyone without a supply to share out. Such was the life-style of a Sun conjunct Neptune and Moon in Pisces person.

Both of these issues did prove to be of major importance over the time he was in therapy with me.

Let us go back to the issue of money, the second house, and how that ties in to his values and self-worth. When Jack began his therapy he was working as a homosexual prostitute. He wanted a lot of money, the second house, the strong Libra energy of being for others, of giving to others, the Virgo rising of being of service and the Mercury conjunct Jupiter in Scorpio, opportunity, expansion, amoral, underworld, sex – he inhabited a strange world.

With the Pluto transit to his Venus and Sun he was beginning to find his work increasingly objectionable. In the past he had travelled extensively, Mars in the ninth house, and stayed in expensive hotels living a life of luxury as part of his work, being a companion and providing sexual services. These days his work was far less glamorous and he was beginning to get in touch with his anger and contempt for his 'punters' as he called them, not wishing to oblige them, all as Pluto crossed his Sun in Libra. He frequently suffered with his infected tooth after bouts of work, but he had still not managed to let go of this work as a way of earning what he saw as easy money.

By May 1984, Pluto was back on his Sun for the third time. At this point he developed a rash that covered his entire body. It was diagnosed as a fungal infection that was virtually untreatable and that would take about nine weeks to run its course and clear. He particularly minded the disfigurement, and in fact the scabs left white mottled marks on him that took about a year to fade. He said his whole summer was blighted and felt he could not go out in daylight, all classic Pluto transit stuff that we have seen time and time again. In some way a person is immobilised and forced to turn inwards, to spend time alone and reflect, and it seems the outer events that force someone to turn inwards reflect the extent to which they resist.

But what was most important about his rash was that he had to stop his work. He could not take his clothes off, and no one would want to touch him. He had already known that he needed to stop, but had not, and now he was finally forced to.

After a period of depression and acute financial difficulties he found himself a job in a restaurant working as a waiter. It was an expensive and outrageous establishment with a glamorous clientele. Here he was back in the money, he got big tips, and he quickly learned to fiddle the bills (Mercury conjunct Jupiter in Scorpio, Sun conjunct Neptune), as apparently all the staff did.

Here he was introduced to heroin, by other people working with him. This was the beginning of the final descent into hell, beginning with Pluto making its final transit to his Sun and heading for his Neptune.

This was a grim time: he became estranged from his cocaine-taking friends, to whom heroin was unacceptable; he sold a lot of his possessions; he missed more sessions than he made; he got the sack. He worked for a time in other dubious and illegal ways, further ingenious manifestations of his Mercury. He left one job after a violent scare. At this point he could not have sunk much lower. He frequently tried to come off heroin, only to slip back. Finally, however, he managed it.

This was the turning-point. At first, all the suicidal feelings in him that he suppressed and acted out by taking heroin began to surface. This was a period of deep understanding and slowly life improved.

At this point he found an organisation which offers sustained support and counselling to ex-addicts, and an ongoing programme of recovery. This organisation has support meetings every evening, and teaches a strong spiritual philosophy. Jack is still actively involved with them and has developed a spiritual philosophy that satisfies his Moon in Pisces and Sun–Neptune conjunction and has helped him stay off drugs. He no longer associates with any of the people he used to regard as friends in his drug-taking days, and has found a new circle of friends.

I want to go back though to the issue of relationships. As Uranus approached to square to his Moon, Jack fell in love with a woman for the first time. It was a very painful time for him as he was, despite all his sexual experience, totally inexperienced in bringing his love feelings together with his sexual feelings in relation to a woman. While this relationship was doomed on a practical level, as she was involved elsewhere, in terms of growth it was extremely important as his love feelings for a woman had been awakened, and he subsequently understood a lot more about himself, and his relationship to his mother.

As you would expect with a Moon in Pisces, he idealised his mother. She was on a pedestal and he had identified with her and all her suffering and had never questioned the way he had been treated.

His mother is someone who could not cope with the demands of a large family and who would lash out violently at them in an attempt to avoid falling apart herself. When Jack came into therapy he had no awareness of what her unpredictable violent attacks on him throughout his childhood had done to him. For him it was normal to be hit (Moon opposite Pluto in a T-square to Mars). He had nevertheless become extremely frightened and he had suppressed his fear as that made his mother worse. The only time he could be upset was if she was; otherwise his being upset only aggravated the situation.

His father had his own business and escaped the rather turbulent home-life by working ten or more hours a day, leaving his wife to manage the children. He virtually abdicated any responsibility (Sun in the second house conjunct Neptune).

During his therapy he began to realise the extent to which his childhood had been traumatic, in particular in that he never allowed himself to feel his fear, hurt and anger on an everyday level.

He began to accept his feelings and to trace them back to their roots in his childhood, to piece together what made him who he was today and to free himself from the grip these early experiences still wielded on him.

This is signified by Saturn conjunct the IC as well as the Moon–Mars–Pluto T-square.

I stopped seeing him regularly once he found the drug dependency organisation as they have an all-embracing programme, with their own counsellors. From a therapeutic point of view, our relationship was not resolved.

Soon after he stopped using heroin he got a job with a communications company, another manifestation of his Mercury. He has worked his way up in this company to become its managing director, and has made the most tremendous success of this position, doubling the company's turnover each year.

He has also been a leading light within the drugs dependency organisation and chaired many meetings, organised events, and generally inspired others. As Pluto transited his Mercury–Jupiter conjunction, he was deeply involved in public speaking describing his own experiences. Everything in his life seemed to be going so well, a real transformational story.

In November 1988 he contacted me to do his Solar Return and told me he was HIV positive. He had been in hospital with an Aids-related illness earlier that year but was feeling well now. The questions he asked at that time were about relationships; he was in love with a woman.

Figure 9.2 is his Solar Return for 1988 to 1989. The following analysis follows the sequence we describe in Chapter 5.

(1) The Sun is in the eleventh house in his Solar Return. This will make groups, and him finding his place within groups, an important focus of his energy. He will be discovering more of who he is through group interactions.

Knowing, as we do that Jack is already deeply involved with group activities in his commitment to the drugs dependency organisation, then we would expect this year to be particularly significant in terms of this involvement. He is already an important member of this group. In his work, too, as managing director, he is a group leader, and

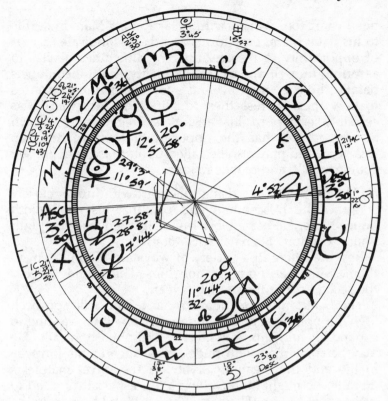

Fig. 9.2. Jack's Solar Return 22.10.88

there may be developments within his work that enhance his feeling of importance.

This house placement also indicates a focus on future plans, and the fulfilling of dreams and ideals. Jack took flying lessons this year, to fulfil a childhood ambition to be a pilot. This is discussed more later, as it is significant in other ways as well.

The Sun is sextile Uranus and Saturn, and this indicates the possibility of some fundamental change in his identity, prompted by an attempt to find a resolution to the tension and frustration he will be experiencing. Even more importantly, the Sun is inconjunct Mars, an aspect he has in his natal chart too, which, with Solar Return Mars in sextile to his natal Mars, now forms a yod. This indicates a year of opportunity to resolve inherent difficulties he has in asserting himself and his individuality. With inconjuncts natally there is often a blind spot within the person as to how they express these qualities. In Jack there was certainly a gap in his awareness regarding his own aggression. He has the opportunity to close this gap this year, and may also be called upon to express himself courageously, and to take risks.

(2) He has Sagittarius rising this year, with Jupiter closely conjunct the Descendant and conjunct his natal ninth house Mars. He has a Libra MC, with Venus in the ninth house, conjunct his natal Ascendant.

Repeated here in a variety of ways are the interwoven themes of travel and of relationships. This is undoubtedly the second major theme of the year.

The Sagittarius Ascendant indicates he will approach life with optimism and confidence. He will be wanting to expand his horizons both literally and philosophically. He may be concerned with huge issues such as his purpose in life and the meaning of life. If the travel manifests literally, he might be travelling a lot, especially abroad to places new to him. His natal Pluto is closely squaring the Ascendant – Descendant axis, which indicates considerable intensity in his approach to life and to relationships. Relationships are likely to be dramatic and to bring a lot of growth and change. This whole theme is extremely charged and volatile. Jupiter is conjunct his natal Mars, which is the focal planet in his T-square, so all these complicated emotions are being channelled into the area of personal relationships.

The Libra MC symbolises the goals and ambitions of the year, in relation to the Sun. This could be seen as a need to achieve justice, balance and harmony within all the eleventh house spheres in which he participates.

Venus, ruling the MC, is in Virgo in the ninth house showing discrimination and selectivity in how he relates to others, and pleasure and happiness possibly derived from learning, travel or personal growth. He might love someone of a different culture, or enjoy studying or visiting places that expand his consciousness in some way. With the Sun in the eleventh, this might be a group travel, or group study. We have repeated here a similar theme to Jupiter on the Descendant, re-emphasising the symbolism that pertains to both significators. Venus is also conjunct his natal Ascendant, which indicates that his quest for leisure and pleasure will permeate the way he ordinarily approaches life. His main priority will be relating to others and he will be popular within the ninth house spheres of activities he chooses to pursue.

(3) The Moon is in Pisces, the same sign as it is in natally, and in the third house. This indicates a need for mental stimulation, with a likelihood of Jack being pulled in different directions by a variety of interests, with a high level of restlessness.

It is possible he will be studying, particularly with the Sun in the eleventh too; he could well be going on courses from which he derives a lot of satisfaction.

We know he has recently moved into a new neighbourhood and would expect him to be settling into this, generally exploring it and finding his place.

This placement also indicates the possibility of some difficulty or issue with a brother or sister being dealt with during the course of the year.

The Moon, in the same sign as it is in natally, is very significant and will give him a feeling of emotional safety and easiness, as he is responding in a familiar mode. Thus, he will be sensitive, sympathetic and compassionate. He may still balk at the demands of everyday life, and wish to escape or for something out of the ordinary to occur.

The Moon is conjunct the natal Descendant, re-emphasising the need for a relationship and for a considerable depth of closeness with someone. It is in a T-square, in close opposition to Venus and widely square Uranus and Saturn. The Moon is sesquiquadrate Venus in the natal chart, so this opposition represents the opportunity to become more aware of his inherent inner conflicts concerning relationships. That this opposition falls across his natal angles brings it to the foreground, and re-emphasises that relationships are of prime concern. It is closely square his natal IC and Saturn, showing the degree of difficulty he is currently experiencing in his relating, and how deeply rooted in his early painful childhood experiences his current difficulties are.

The squares to Saturn and Uranus indicate difficulties and frustrations in his contact with others. These planets are deep into the first house, and indicate that his approach, beneath the optimistic and confident Sagittarius exterior, is a lot more tense and fraught than it at first appears. Contacting Venus and the Moon will mean this is particularly so in his contact with women. He has a major challenge here: he wants closeness, but he is extremely tetchy and difficult to relate to.

(4) The house emphasis is on angular houses. He has five planets in angular houses, two in succedent, and three in cadent. This re-emphasises the mutable, cardinal Angles, and gives an overview to the year as one that contains a mixture of new beginnings and of adjustment to existing circumstances. The year will be marked by a sense of preparation for something that follows, as well as projects and relationships beginning this year.

(5) The main aspect pattern within the Solar Return is the T-square, which we have already discussed.

Mercury is in Libra and in the tenth house. This is a good career indication, as he works in a Mercurial business, and could indicate new deals and negotiations going on. This is a diplomatic and gracious placement, and shows skill in making deals. This could also indicate travel for business purposes, of an ordinary and everyday kind. There is a wide trine to Jupiter, and Mercury rules the Descendant and is the dispositor of Jupiter, so more romantic and exotic travel comes back into the picture.

Mars also needs further consideration. This is an extremely powerful position for Mars, just into Aries, a sign it rules. The First Point of Aries is a birth moment; its close conjunction with the IC, the most unconscious point in the chart indicates a deep and psychological battle, a primitive and instinctual fight, possibly one of survival. In the consultation in November of 1988, Jack told me he was having flying lessons and that it had been a childhood ambition to be a pilot. That he should learn to fly, with all that it symbolises for him, fits a lot of the chart significators. The Ascendant is close to 5 degrees of Sagittarius, an important degree for aviation, and Jupiter is opposite this. Childhood ambitions are also signified by an eleventh house Sun, but in particular Mars on an Aries IC signifies the daring and courage he wanted to test within himself. When I later spoke with him he had decided to stop flying because it frightened him too much. You could say he decided he did not want to dice with death, and he felt afraid of the prospect.

(6) Next we will look at planets that are in aspect to each other within the natal chart that are also in aspect within the Solar Return. These are listed in Figure 9.3.

We have already discussed the Sun inconjunct Mars. This is probably the most important repeated aspect, as not only is it the same aspect but both the natal Mars and the Solar Return Mars are angular. The opportunity to remedy a long-term existing predisposition is optimum.P

The Moon opposing Venus has also been touched on in relation to his natal Moon Venus sesquiquadrate. This is a rather unconscious aspect, that people tend to have little awareness of wheras an opposition is in its essence an aspect of awareness. There is the opportunity for Jack to become far more aware of long-standing inconsistencies within himself in his attitudes to relationships, and his everyday well-being and happiness. He may become more in touch with how he sabotages things for himself. He has conflicting desires and therefore gives ambivalent messages to others. He can use this year to learn a lot about these inner conflicts, as they will be more accessible to him now, as not only are these planets in sharp opposition, but they are conjunct the natal Ascendant–Descendant axis.

Solar Return			Natal Chart		
☉	⚹	♂	☉	⚹	♂
☽	☍	♀	☽	⯐	♀
☽	Q	♆	☽	△	♆
☿	△	♃	☿	☌	♃
☿	□	♇	☿	☌	♇
♀	□	♇	♀	✳	♇
♇	♂	♅	♇	△	♅
♆	✳	♇	♆	✳	♇

Fig. 9.3. Planets in aspect to each other in both the Solar Return
and the natal chart.

The Moon is trine Neptune in his natal chart, and quintile Neptune in his Solar Return. There is an openness and emotional vulnerability that permeates Jack's existence, that continues throughout this year. The quintile is an aspect of instinctual knowledge, so we could expect that he has the potential to 'know' more about this dimension of himself this year.

Mercury is conjunct Jupiter natally and trine Jupiter in his Solar Return. This Mercury–Jupiter conjunction has manifested as the opportunist in Jack and given him the facility to land on his feet, and turn himself around with remarkable dexterity. In more recent times he has had a lot of success as managing directer of his company, and as a powerful public speaker, able to reach a great many people emotionally. The trine this year indicates these successful themes within his life are continuing without any effort on his part. The wheels have been set in motion and things just roll along. There is nothing new or spectacular here, just a continuation of what he is best at.

Mercury is also conjunct Neptune natally and square Neptune in his Solar Return. The thing that strikes me most about this contact is something Jack said during the consultation. When he had moved into his new flat he had not known he was HIV positive, and he was saying how if he had known he would not have been able to buy the flat, as no one would have lent him the money for the mortgage and he would have been unable to get life assurance. He was commenting on how fortunate his timing had been, as while on some level he had known, it was of utmost importance to him that he was not at least consciously aware of it at that point, since he could not have lied about it as he now felt a need to be totally honest in everything. Although this new policy had begun before this Solar Return, this greater awareness of his previous use of lies to get out of awkward situations, or to get what he wanted, is signified by the square this year.

Venus is sextile Saturn natally and is square Saturn in this year's Solar Return. This will bring into sharper focus inherent difficulties Jack has in relating to others. While he does not seem shy or awkward, in fact he has considerable problems in making satisfactory intimate relationships, and tends to erect barriers between himself and others that protect him from hurt but prevent genuine contact. With a natal sextile aspect he can avoid confronting this problem, but that does not mean it goes away, it just never gets properly looked at or resolved. With Venus and Saturn in square this year there is the opportunity to make considerable progress with these difficulties as they are thrust into the foreground and he is forced to grapple with them. They are made even more obvious and apparent because his natal Ascendant is conjunct Venus in the Solar Return.

Saturn is trine Uranus in Jack's natal chart and they are conjunct in his Solar Return. This is helpful. He will be inherently innovative and progressive in his attitudes and ideas, and throughout the time of this conjunction the opportunity for him to implement his ideas will be at its peak. He could make progress in many directions where original thought can be used in a practical way to improve things.

Neptune is sextile Pluto in his natal chart and his Solar Return. These planets have been in sextile to each other since the early 1940s so this has very little personal significance for Jack as no one born since then has any experience of these planets not being in sextile.

(7) We will now look at planets that fall in the same signs in the natal chart and Solar Return, as well as planets in the Solar Return that aspect themselves in the natal chart.

The Moon is in Pisces both in the natal chart and Solar Return. This has already been touched on earlier and indicates an ease in Jack in how he responds and reacts throughout this year. On some level he is at one with himself, and despite other stressful factors, this indicates that he will be feeling at his most certain and secure. This will stand him in good stead and give him the inner confidence to tackle some of his difficulties.

Neither Mercury nor Venus are in the signs that they are in natally. In these areas he does not have an ease; rather he is being stretched. In his relating he is exploring new territory, and is not at all on safe ground. In his thinking and communicating he is more aware of how he comes across, more diplomatic and prepared to negotiate and compromise, in order to get what he wants. Mercury is in the same sign as his Sun, so he is likely to be learning mostly about himself.

Mars in the Solar Return is in sextile to Mars in his natal chart. This is a helpful aspect with regard to self-assertion. He has an easy access to his natural way of asserting himself, so in all areas where he needs to fight, or to establish himself, he will be assisted by being able to summon up his innate strengths. This sextile forms a yod formation with Jack's Sun, so is further emphasised. Self-assertion, survival, is a critical issue this year, and through the Sun, connects to his identity and individuality.

(8) Finally we will look at the aspects between the planets and Angles in the Solar Return chart to the planets and Angles in the natal chart. These are listed in Figure 9.4. We have discussed most of these contacts already.

Solar Return		Natal Chart
☽	♂	Desc
☽	☐	♄
☽	☐	I.c.
☿	♂	♆
♀	♂	Asc
♀	☐	♄
♀	☐	I.c.
♃	♂	♂
Desc	♂	♂

Fig. 9.4. Aspects between the planets and Angles in the Solar Return to the planets and Angles in the natal chart.

Pluto is conjunct natal Mercury. This is a separating transit, and relates to Jack's passionate belief in the drug dependency organisation's programme of recovery which led him to speak in public and to chair meetings. This falls in the eleventh house of his Solar Return and indicates a continuing involvement, that may wain as the year progresses and Pluto moves on.

When Jack contacted me to arrange the consultation in which we looked at this Solar Return, the main issue he enquired about was relationships. He was in love with a woman and wanted to ask more about this. This, as a main theme in the year, is clearly described, but is an area fraught with difficulties and obstacles. Within the relationship Jack failed to feel sexual feelings towards her, and the prospect filled him with terror and pain. While he felt a lot for her, he could not allow himself to get that close. He has subsequently ended his involvement with her and returned to a homosexual relationship which is less threatening and more rewarding for him. The year clearly shows a testing time, in which something major will be resolved concerning relationships.

His involvement with the drugs dependency organisation was important, and he did become something of a leader within the organisation. As well as chairing many meetings he acted as an inspiration to other newer members.

Friendships were very important; he made new friends within the organisation, who shared his ideals, and were focused on the same goals. He also made a new friend who helped him realise long-held aims within his work.

The question of his health was not something he enquired about, and yet, knowing he is HIV positive and had been ill earlier that year with an Aids-related illness, one is bound to wonder, and consider what the nature of the journeys and travel might be that the chart clearly indicates. When the progressed MC conjuncted Jupiter he went on a holiday to Spain with a group of friends, which was not entirely satisfactory for him. Apart from this the whole year contained an enormous amount of business travel, which he enjoyed at first and managed to combine with pleasure, but began to find really exhausting. The degree of stress he was under gave him concern for his health, and he decided to limit his travel.

There is a close Chiron–Neptune opposition across the second–eighth house axis. This might also cause concern regarding his health. In reality he is extremely well, and the virus is entirely dormant. The uncomfortable first house seems to have related to him being more aware of the stress he was under and implementing changes to reduce this, and thereby protect his vitality (the sextiles to his Sun). This is an extremely constructive use of the potential shown in the chart, and perhaps goes with the constructive use of his Mars on the IC, to protect his survival, and his angular Jupiter in his use of his intuition.

Using the timing methods described in Chapter 6, we would expect the time when the Moon by progression made exact squares to Uranus and Saturn to be critical in terms of relationships, and again as it inconjuncts the Sun and conjuncts Mars, in terms of his need to assert his individuality. The squares to Uranus and Saturn occurred throughout April. His heterosexual relationship had ended and he was back to feeling more reconciled to being gay.

The Moon reached the inconjunct to the Sun by mid-May, and its conjunction to Mars by the end of May. It conjuncted the IC in mid-June. Throughout this period he was abroad a lot, and re-established friendships with people he had known over ten years before. This also was the point at which he recognised that the amount of travelling he was doing was stressful.

Progressing the MC as described in Chapter 6, the times we would think most likely to be significant would be as it crosses the Sun, the Moon and Mars, and later Jupiter. These are possibly critical dates during the year, in which key events connected to the themes of the chart might manifest. In retrospective discussion with Jack, when the MC crossed the Sun on 19 November 1988 he was in the process of renegotiating his status and salary at work. He had, up until then, been working on a self-employed basis, and changed to being employed directly by the company. This made his position more secure.

The MC crossed the Moon on 9 April and Mars on the 18th. This month has already been picked out as important as the progressed Moon is making exact squares to Saturn and Uranus, so these dates may be particularly significant for key events regarding relationships. On both these dates Jack was abroad on business, and enjoying the old friends he had met up with again. On the 15th he began a new relationship, with someone who lived abroad. This was short-lived, but important for him.

The MC crossed Jupiter on 25 June, and this would signify a key time in terms of its symbolism, when some tangible outer expression might be visible. This coincided with a holiday in Spain that Jack went on with a group of friends. He described himself as feeling very torn and dissatisfied. He felt he was not where he wanted to be, or with the people he wanted to be with. They were miles from anywhere in the mountains, and he felt very restless and wanted to go off somewhere else. This is a not untypical rather negative Jupiterean feeling, particularly the itching to move on to greener pastures.

Looking at a sequence of his Lunar Returns, shown in Figures 9.5, 9.6, 9.7 and 9.8, we can see at a glance, from angular planets, months that stand out, and months which look quieter. His Lunar Return for April looks the most dynamic month and February's looks the quietest. This is the third way that the month of April has been shown to be important.

His February's Lunar Return has virtually the same Angles as his natal chart, which means the Moon is in the same house as it is in natally. This is a familiar area of life that he continually grapples with emotionally.

This month may be one where work dominates, and where most emotional satisfaction comes from the work he is engaged in. In Jack's case it could be financial satisfaction, as this matters to him a lot.

There is likely to be a preoccupation in creating personal daily routines that support his well-being. This will include things like making sure he gets regular meals, enough exercise, relaxation and sleep. He may enjoy paying attention to these areas of his life during this month. There are no angular planets, so it is not likely to be experienced as an important time, that stands out in any dramatic way, rather a low-key time of preparation.

Jack says his relationship with his woman friend ended at this time, and as she had virtually lived in his flat we can see how he would be re-establishing his routines.

March looks much more dramatic, with Uranus closely conjunct the MC and Neptune and Saturn nearby. Here we would expect him to feel intense frustration around any compromises he has made, and to be making a strong bid to get things how he wants them to be. This could be to do with his career, or it could involve goals he has within his personal life.

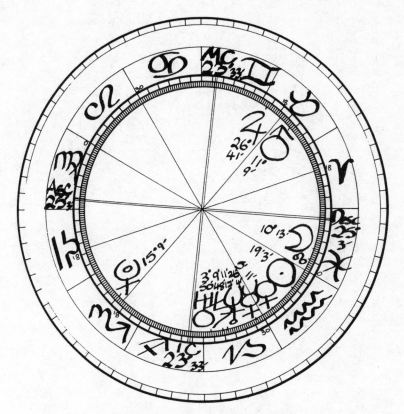

Fig. 9.5. Jack's Lunar Return 7.2.89

There is a New Moon in this Lunar Return, hidden away in the twelfth. Some new phase of introspection and solitude is beginning as that is what he needs most at the moment. Something has come to a head, and he needs time to withdraw and sift through his feelings. It is likely that he will experience things as particularly complicated and confusing in his relating to women, and it may signify that a friendship has recently ended. We now know this to be the case.

April is a key month, with five angular planets. Saturn and Neptune are conjunct the IC and the Sun, Mercury and Venus are all closely conjunct the Descendant. A month

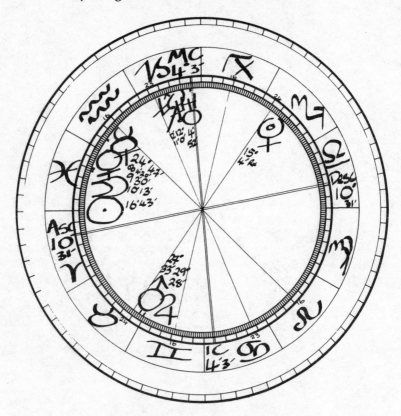

Fig. 9.6. Jack's Lunar Return 7.3.89

such as this we would expect to stand out and probably to contain outer events.

With Saturn and Neptune on the IC we would expect him to be rather reclusive. He may find his contact with others is not profound or meaningful enough and he may prefer to spend time alone to contemplate and day-dream. He may feel rather lonely, having doubts, anxieties and insecurities connected to his personal life. He may be reflecting on his past. There may be practical problems and discomfort within his home.

The rest of the Lunar Return gives a rather different picture. With the Sun, Mercury and Venus all conjunct his

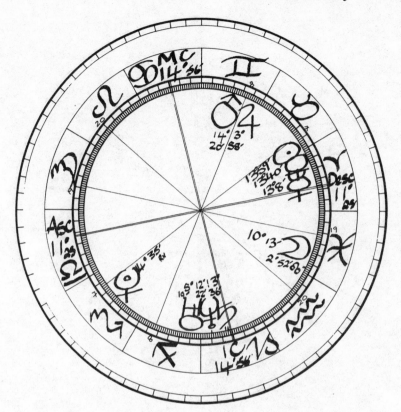

Fig. 9.7. Jack's Lunar Return 3.4.89

Descendant, coupled with a fifth house Moon, this looks like a very sociable time where he will be noticed and receive a lot of attention. This might be a situation where despite the love and appreciation showered on him he still feels lonely inside, or aware of an inner emptiness that is not necessarily to do with his current life. He has Saturn on the IC in his natal chart, so he could be re-experiencing the loneliness from his childhood, accentuated this month by things going very well. There could easily be the start of a new relationship, or some significant change in an existing one.

In fact he was abroad a lot, mixing business and

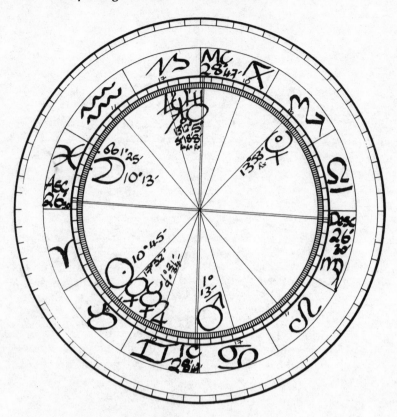

Fig. 9.8. Jack's Lunar Return 1.5.89

pleasure, and going to glitzy parties with show-business contacts. He was back again to feeling more reconciled to being gay and started a new relationship.

The May Lunar Return has the Moon back in the twelfth, with the Lunar Return Ascendant conjunct his natal Descendant. This is a contemplative time, with relationships still emphasised. The Sun is closely sextile the Moon, so he is likely to feel reasonably at ease within himself. However, Pluto, Saturn and Neptune all link in with the Sun and Moon to form challenges and opportunities, so things will not be that smooth. Their aspects to the Moon are all harmonious, perhaps intensifying the introspective phase he is in and at times making him more melancholic. In this case the close square to Jupiter is likely to increase his dissatisfactions and restlessness.

Mars is closely conjunct the IC, as it is in his Solar Return, so we would expect the whole theme around primitive survival issues and how able or not he is to be self-assertive, to be particularly important this month. This placement could describe him feeling angry about old wounds, injuries and grievances that are being dredged up from the past.

Uranus is widely conjunct the MC, so again frustration about not getting what he wants on a personal level is likely to be felt, and he may act unpredictably in an attempt to satisfy his needs.

From what we now know his new relationship was already coming to an end. This was the month he met a new colleague who was to become a friend who helped him realise aims within his work. It was the month when his travelling began to ease up.

Let us move on to more recent times, and look at Jack's Solar Return for 1989 to 1990 shown in Figure 9.9. We will follow the same sequence for interpreting Solar Returns that we used earlier.

The Sun is in the seventh house this year, continuing the relationship theme that was emphasised in last year's Solar Return. This year the focus is on learning about himself through others, through close personal relationships, through counselling, or through direct conflict, one way or another and possibly through all these ways, Jack will be encountering new aspects of himself hitherto unknown to him. Jack has innate relationship difficulties (Venus sextile Saturn, Moon opposite Pluto), in particular in allowing himself to be vulnerable, and his tendency is to try to keep the upper hand, and maintain control of the relationship. The Sun in the seventh will bring to his attention any inequalities within existing relationships, and he may feel used and exploited, and as a consequence question his relating patterns. The Sun is sextile Uranus, which

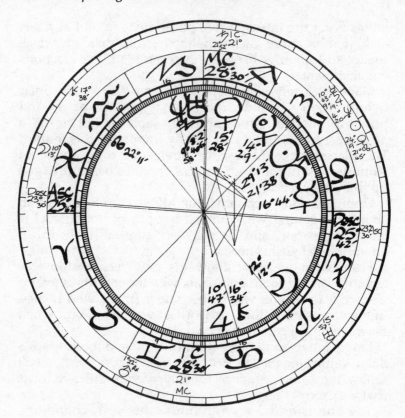

Fig. 9.9. Jack's Solar Return for 1989–90

means the opportunity is there to bring about changes in himself, through his relating, which will increase his sense of self-esteem.

The Sun in the seventh house also signifies a year when he is likely to get more public attention. It is a time when he could be in the limelight, getting attention and appreciation from others. This is likely to give him greater confidence in himself.

The Sun is semi-square Venus, underlining the importance of relationships and the struggle he will be experiencing in this area of life. He has a Sun–Venus conjunction natally, so having them semi-square this year brings with it the opportunity for him to have more perspective on his relationships patterns, to be able to assess them and have a more objective view of himself.

The Sun is also widely conjunct Mars, which is a superb opportunity for him to be more aware of the assertive side of himself, and of how he comes across. In his natal chart these planets are inconjunct, so Jack tends to be rather blind to how forceful he can appear to others, but this year, with the planets conjunct and in the seventh house, he will be very aware of others' responses to him, and subsequently more aware of himself.

The Angles of this Solar Return are remarkable in that they are the natal Angles reversed: the Ascendant is conjunct the natal Descendant. This underlines yet again that relationships are to the forefront. With Pisces rising, his approach to life will be fluid, unformed, changeable, sensitive and receptive. Neptune, the modern ruler of Pisces, is in the tenth house, closely conjunct Saturn and opposite Jupiter. This gives an emphasis on his career, with the possibility of him concretising a dream; of bringing a vision, held in his imagination, into reality. This is the configuration which, exactly three weeks later, symbolised the dismantling of the Berlin Wall and a new beginning in the East, and in East–West relations. In some way a wall is being dismantled inside Jack, and a greater inner freedom and choice will transpire. This could be in his career, or his aspirations, in his home, in his relationship to his parents, both now and in how he understands his childhood and past, or in his private and inner psychological self. Jupiter, in the fourth house and exalted in Cancer, is the ruler of the MC, and is the traditional ruler of Pisces, this year's Ascendant. From this we would place the emphasis of this opposition on his inner private world, and on his home-life. We would think there will be some very constructive breakthrough for him, which has an expansive effect on him psychologically.

The Sagittarius MC indicates expansion of consciousness from either inner growth or outer travel. Given what we know of Jack this is likely to be both. He tends to travel a lot and, regarding inner growth, this is a path he is already committed to. His need for philosophical understanding is particularly emphasised, and will take him back, through Jupiter, to his past and inner life. Uranus, in Capricorn, is conjunct the Sagittarius MC, and this gives an alarming and unpredicatable quality to where he might be headed this year. It has the feel of total freedom from all worldly constraints; it is essentially a signifier of the free spirit. One would expect any constraints placed upon Jack, particularly those he sees as serving no purpose, to become intolerable to him. His need for scope, and to do what he wants when he wants, is strongly stated. He could also become quite autocratic himself as a boss, losing tolerance that he once had, as he wants what he wants straight away. This is in contrast to other dynamics within the chart, but supports certain blind spots he has as far as being assertive is concerned (natal Sun inconjunct Mars).

The Saturn conjunct Neptune opposite Jupiter is also widely square Mercury, in Libra and in the seventh house. Mercury is also the ruler of the Descendant. Here the need for one-to-one relating and communication is emphasised. Earlier we said with Mercury in the same sign as the Sun you may be learning about yourself. Here Jack is clearly learning about himself in relation to others. He may find himself a link person, mediating between others, and having to use his skills in diplomacy to the utmost.

The Moon is in Leo and in the sixth house, the same house the Moon occupies in the natal chart. This re-emphasises his need to pay attention to his health and to the ordinary routines and rituals of everyday life, making sure he does not become over-stressed. Work is also signified, with the likelihood that he will be deriving considerable emotional satisfaction from his work, and from his relationship to his colleagues. In Leo, there is a need for attention, to be of significance and to be at the centre of things. The danger here is that he will gain the feeling of being special through ill health. More constructively he may be receiving this attention through his work. He is already a managing director, which is an important role, and it could be he particularly enjoys the prestige this year. What he needs is a way of being important, of being in the limelight in some way, or in someone's eyes, within the context of everyday life. Given that the Sun is in the seventh, emphasising relationships, the need for an important relationship, where Jack feels special and important, could be one way to interpret this placement. Another scenario could be him joining a prestigious gym, where he meets influential people as he works out and has a massage, and following the seventh house Sun slant, he attempts to establish equal relationships.

The Moon is applying to a close square to Pluto, and by progression it will be exact over Christmas 1989 and the New Year. We would expect that time to be emotionally difficult and complicated. He might feel quite lonely and isolated, walled off inside himself and protecting himself from hurt. He may have chosen to be alone, badly needing some space just to be with himself. He could, alternatively, feel invaded and overwhelmed, there not being enough space. Whichever way this manifests, the events of this time symbolise important inner dynamics that Jack has to struggle with continually, as he has Moon opposite Pluto in his natal chart. This may mean he will gain more understanding of his early relationship with his mother, and how she invaded him, and how that still affects him, particularly in the way he tries to maintain control in relationships, thus preventing others from getting really close to him.

The Moon is trine Venus and both are sextile Mercury. This is a happy and fortunate configuration, and will give an ease and enjoyment in his relating, particularly with women, and an enjoyment in communicating and sharing his feelings. This is extremely helpful to have alongside the challenging square to Pluto and offers an opportunity to make real progress in his relating, and free himself from some of the limitations from his childhood.

The Moon is also widely conjunct his natal Uranus, and square his natal Jupiter–Mercury conjunction. This natal square describes a side to Jack that is 'footloose and fancy-free' and enjoys shocking others. There's a lot of sheer mischief in this configuration. That the Moon is picking up on this means he will be responding to others in an extremely frank way. His need for emotional excitement and stimulation will be strong. He will want to break free of emotional constraints, and may behave in an unpredictable way. He could be positively outrageous, as the natal planets have this propensity, and the Moon, in Leo, may go right overboard to get attention. Whatever, life will not be dull.

There is a strong emphasis on the angular houses, seven planets in all being in angular houses, with only two in cadent houses and one in a succedent house. There is also an emphasis on cardinality, although the angles are all mutable. The feel is of someone who appears a lot more flexible and adaptable than he actually is, and that in fact he is very driven, with a strong sense of his goals and priorities, from which he will not waver. He is far more focused than he appears, and his apparent fluidity will be to serve his more defined aims, which are primarily personal and private.

The main aspect pattern of this year's Solar Return is the cardinal T-square, which we have already discussed quite a lot. Mercury is the focal planet and this puts all communication under considerable strain. Jack is likely to feel misunderstood, and despite his attempts to be diplomatic and congenial he is likely to convey an impatience and irritability in his contacts with others. Mars is conjunct Mercury, so he may be positively argumentative. Competition creeps in here, and he may want to score points. Winning is important to him, and some outlet where he can compete for all he's worth, and really beat the other person, is needed. Squash or tennis spring to mind, or possibly mind games like scrabble or chess. These would give him an alternative outlet for these energies so that they do not disrupt his personal relating. Mars is closely conjunct his natal north node, and widely conjunct natal Venus. This contact could work very positively for him in so far as he will have 'winning ways' in his relating, with considerable charm and a dynamic flair. He brings a lot of energy and concern to all his relating so he is likely to get away with being a little brusque at times. He is likely to be keenly aware of what he wants, and it may be that what he wants is money, as the north node and Venus are both in the second house natally, and he may be grappling with how his wealth and desire for money affect his relationships, and with what his true values are. He may find qualities in others he desires, that cannot be bought.

This whole configuration in Libra could also relate to a new awareness in him about his capacity to over-accommodate others and compromise himself. This would be rooted in his need for others' approval, coupled with low self-esteem, and this year he may begin to love and value himself more. This would give him a stronger sense of his identity and worth and help him enjoy better, more equal relationships with others.

Venus is in Sagittarius and in the ninth house, which gives an idealistic and hopeful attitude to love and relationships. He had Venus in the ninth house last year (in Virgo) so this is a continuing theme. Pleasure and happiness may be found through travel or a learning situation. He may derive enjoyment through philosophical study, or make friends this way, this could relate to his continuing involvement with the drugs dependency organisation, which teaches a spiritual philosophy. Many of his friends are a part of this organisation, and this would indicate that he will continue to enjoy spending his leisure time participating in the organisation. Venus is closely trine his natal Uranus, which will increase the idealism of this placement as well as his need for freedom and excitement. He will not make any emotional commitments easily this year.

Jupiter in the Solar Return is exactly trine his natal Moon, and the Saturn–Neptune conjunction is sextile his natal Moon. This Solar Return opposition has already been discussed, but having it picked up by his natal Moon, that falls in the Solar Return's twelfth house, further emphasises the inner, private nature of its likely manifestation, and that it concerns him in re-evaluating his past and childhood, and how that affects his current home and personal life, as well as his career.

Uranus in his Solar Return is applying to trine Pluto. Pluto, in the natal twelfth house, describes his inner capacity to change, and to draw on innate resources when needed, as well as his tendency to carry, and be attempting to redeem, the psychic pain of his whole family. The Uranus trine energises in a dynamic way this whole dilemma, and with Uranus conjunct the MC, one could say this is of major concern, and something he focuses on and makes a priority of this year.

Conversely, Pluto in the Solar Return is square natal Uranus. These contacts are ones of profound, slow change. Uranus is in the eleventh house natally, so this would re-emphasise the theme of friendship that is shown this year. Pluto is in the eighth in the Solar Return, which suggests that some kind of death, in order that something new can form, will be going on. This could be in his attitudes to intimacy, or money, or sex. Whatever, it will affect friendships.

Finally, we want to look at planets that are in aspect to each other in both the Solar Return and the natal chart. Some of these have already been mentioned, so we will only look at those we have not already picked up on. These, as well as the aspects between the planets and Angles in the Solar Return and the planets and Angles in the natal chart, which we have just discussed, are all listed in Figures 9.10 and 9.11.

The Moon's sextile to Mercury in the Solar Return will feel very similar to the trine he has natally. There is an ease within him in communicating his feelings that will continue.

The Moon trine Venus this year follows an opposition he had between these planets last year, when he is likely to have developed an increased awareness of some of his inherent difficulties in relating shown by the sesqui-quadrate in his natal chart. A Moon–Venus sesquiquadrate

Solar Return		Natal Chart
☽	♂	♅
♀	△	♅
♂	♂	♌
♂	♂	♀
♃	△	☽
♄	✳	☽
♆	✳	☽
♅	△	♆
♇	☐	♇

Fig. 9.10. Aspects between planets in the Solar Return and planets
in the natal chart.

tends to be over-accommodating, as one feels essentially
insecure about being lovable, and hence feels acutely one's
need for love and approval. People with this contact are
often popular simply because they make so much effort
to please, but they often pay a high inner price. With
these planets in trine this year he is likely to feel loved
without him having to make an effort, for just being who
he is, which may help heal some of his deeper feelings of
a lack of self-worth.

Mercury, focal in the T-square in the Solar Return, is
square both Jupiter and Neptune, planets it conjuncts in
the natal chart. Mercury was square Neptune last year,
and Jack was already re-evaluating the way he had used
this conjunction until recently to get what he wanted, or
to get out of tight corners. The whole pattern is in even
sharper focus here and will enable him to have more
perspective and awareness with regard to the part of
him earlier described as 'the opportunist'. This is an
extremely creative force within him, and configured here
with Saturn too, could be applied in a practical way.

	Solar Return			**Natal Chart**	
☉	L	♀	☉	♂	♀
☉	♂	♂w	☉	⚹	♂
☽	✶	☿	☽	△	☿
☽	△	♀	☽	⊡	♀
☽	□	♇	☽	☍	♆
☿	□	♃	☿	♂	♃
☿̣☿	□	♆	☿̣☿	♂	♆
♃	☍	♆	♃	♂	♆
♄	♂	♅	♄	△	♅

Fig. 9.11. Planets in aspect to each other in both the Solar Return and the natal chart.

Saturn and Uranus are still conjunct, as they were last year, although separating now, and he has the trine natally. His ability to be innovative, progressive and original and to implement his ideas will continue. As they are in the tenth house this year it is likely he will bring these talents into his work and career.

By progression the Moon squares Pluto over Christmas of 1989. Jack spent this with his mother and said he was aware of her love for him, and of her not wanting to let go of him. As we said earlier, it looks an intense time, with realisations regarding his relationship difficulties. He had begun a new relationship in October, and they were separated briefly over Christmas. His new partner returned to his home country, where Jack visited him just before Christmas. He described this time as especially enjoyable, and said he felt very relaxed and free. Partly he had enjoyed being shown around by his new lover. It seems as if he was already experiencing the progressed Moon's conjunction to natal Uranus and trine to the ninth house Venus. They have become steadily closer and more committed, not something Jack does easily. There also seems to be a lot of excitement in the relationship.

As the progressed Moon sextiles Mercury in mid-March he has read this chapter and been given a different perspective on himself. His mother has also spoken to him on the telephone about him visiting home at a time that will coincide with another sibling visiting.

The progressed Moon will sextile Mars in August and may describe a time in which he will be forthright and direct. Any of the scenarios we described earlier relating to a seventh house Mars could flare up.

The progressed MC conjuncts Jupiter on 2 May 1990 and could indicate a change in his home circumstances. He is considering moving home, yet ambivalent about it, and also considering making changes within his existing home. He could well feel his dissatisfaction very strongly at this time, and take action one way or the other. An opportunity to move may materialise that he cannot resist, but he could just as well be enjoying an expansive time at home.

The progressed MC conjuncts Mercury on 10 August then crosses Mars and gets to the Sun by the 23rd. These planets are configured in all the major themes in this year's Solar Return. Of the possible scenarios they may signify that we have described earlier this will be a key time in their manifestation. How the energies are actually working will become clear at this time as the issues will be sharply defined and highlighted.

Finally, we want to look at Jack's Mercury Return, shown in Figure 9.12, that coincides with this time, to see what that tells us about this year.

We were immediately struck by this chart, with its two stelliums, one in Scorpio in the third house, and the other in Capricorn in the fourth.

To recap, a Mercury Return shows how you process and digest what you learn in that particular year. It shows what your mind will be focused on and how you will approach the whole process of assimilating and disseminating knowledge.

Mercury, in the third house, is the ruler of the Ascendant and MC, and is part of a stellium, being conjunct the Sun

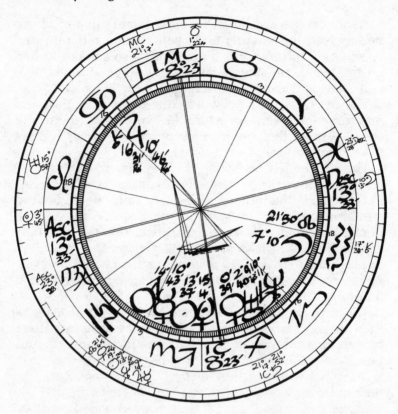

Fig. 9.12. Jack's Mercury Return 6.11.89, 1.26 a.m., GMT, 51°N30′ 0°W7′

and Pluto, and very widely conjunct Mars (technically out of orb). Mercury in the third emphasises restlessness and curiosity. It suggests a time of great mental activity and discovery, delving into all types of experiences that will enhance his knowledge. With Mercury conjunct the Sun, we would expect that he is primarily concerned with self-discovery, and will experiment with anything that might accomplish this. The stellium is in Scorpio, so he will be wanting to explore the depths, to know about his feeling and emotional nature. He may also be curious about other people's inner workings, particularly in so far as it helps him understand himself further. He will be extremely perceptive of others, able to have an accurate feel of where they are really coming from. He will not be fooled by anyone, as he will be able to pick up on anyone trying to lie to him, or just not being above-board in any way. This is an extremely 'sussed' placement. His mind is fast and accurate, and with his keen perception he can wound with words should he choose. He may be good at getting others to tell him their secrets, as he will have a knack of opening others up to talk about private matters and taboo subjects. He may delve into secrets of his own that have been buried and forgotten, and this may affect his understanding of himself. He is likely to begin some new interest this year that profoundly affects his current belief system. This will in some way be transformed during this time, and Jack will create a new framework from which he understands himself and life. This is a deep and radical change, a watershed in his view of the world and how he fits into it.

The third house also describes physical movement, and with the stellium placed here, we would expect Jack to be moving around physically a lot. This could just be him being very restless, and not have any purpose or pattern to it other than to release his agitation. Or it could be more purposeful, and mean he travels about a lot, not to anywhere that he regards as unusual or inspiring, possibly work-connected (Mercury is the ruler of both the Ascendent and MC). Alternatively, he could take up some form of deliberate movement, like dance, or with the depth and power of this particular stellium in Scorpio, some form of martial art. This could suit him very well, and if it is something he has ever considered then now would be a good time to do it.

He could take up writing, in which case he would find it intense and absorbing. It would seem significant that this is the time we are writing about him, and his story is becoming a chapter of a book.

Whatever he takes up, it needs to be something that gives him the opportunity to know himself better in a profound way.

The Ascendant is in Virgo, which he also has natally, which means he is approaching learning in the way he generally approaches life. He will want to understand the purpose of things, how they fit together, how they work, and what makes them useful. He will be evaluating everything according to these criteria and will disregard anything that he does not see any point in. His approach will be methodical, paying close attention to the details and particulars.

Gemini on the MC will make him want to seem versatile and quick in his thinking. He will want others to see him as knowledgeable in a variety of subject areas, and this will in part be his motivation to discover more this year. He will want to know something about everything!

There are conflicts shown by the squares from the stellium to the Moon in Aquarius in the fifth house. The Moon in Aquarius shows him responding in a detached way, of having an innovative and experimental attitude to his feelings, so long as they remain rather impersonal and do not get out of hand. This Moon placement is adventurous, pleasure-seeking and fun-loving, and he may enjoy expressing himself, but it is at odds with his desire to know more about himself psychologically, and may be describing an over-detached perspective that conflicts with a deeper knowledge rooted in feeling experience. It may describe a conflict between self-discovery and pleasure, and they may feel mutually exclusive.

The Moon's squares to Mars and Pluto echo the theme in the natal chart shown by the Moon–Mars–Pluto T-square. He also has the Moon square Pluto in this year's Solar Return. This describes a complex dynamic of intense emotional difficulties. These relate in particular to his trying to maintain control in relationships, to feeling deeply vulnerable and needy at times, and to wanting to avoid facing those feelings. They are shown to be something he will be pushed to deal with within himself over the course of the year, to gain further understanding of how he gets hurt in relationships, of how he perpetuates the painful dynamic.

Let us look at the stellium in Capricorn in the fourth house. There are a lot of sextile aspects between the two stelliums, creating opportunities for the various principles to work well together. Venus is going to describe the kind of contact Jack seeks to make that will facilitate his search for self-knowledge. Venus in Capricorn is often concerned with making relationships that give status or respectability. Capricorn is an eminently conservative sign, but Venus is here closely conjunct Uranus, which indicates that relationships will be full of surprises, and will shock him in some way, or he could behave in a way that shocks. He could also be rather detached, difficult to pin down in any way and reluctant to make any commitments, or else he might be involved with someone like this. The Moon in Aquarius accentuates this theme. Venus and Uranus are both sextile to Mars, adding passion and intensity to what is an unpredictable and unstable combination. It would seem Jack, while in some ways taking a serious and responsible attitude to love and relationships, will nevertheless experience a very changeable and uncertain time in close relationships.

With the fourth house occupied, this could stir up deep and dormant matters. It could also indicate things are very private, and that his relationships are primarily conducted within his home. He will be directing whatever he discovers and learns from his relating to a new understanding of himself (Mercury conjunct Sun in the third house).

Saturn is closely conjunct Neptune and opposite to Jupiter, and the opposition trines and sextiles the Mercury–Sun–Pluto stellium. This opposition was also across the fourth–tenth house axis in his Solar Return, only here Jupiter is elevated. The home, his career, his parents, his inner private world are all signified, with some 'dismantling of walls' indicated. With the opposition channelled through the third house stellium this could be his understanding of these aspects of his life, how they all knit together and affect him, how he is controlled by influences from them. This is an indication of a breakthrough in consciousness, of tremendous potential for liberation from past oppressive forces, possibly that lie dormant within him, the voices from his past that still limit and restrict him. Jupiter is exceedingly well placed, exalted in Cancer, and the most elevated planet, so any breakthroughs he has could bring career opportunities.

There are a lot of contacts between planets in the Mercury Return that he also has in his natal chart. As in his Solar Return, Mercury, Jupiter and Neptune are all configured, only here with trines and sextiles, which indicates a less challenging and stressful relationship between these principles, and yet a continuing opportunity for him to have more perspective.

Mars in the Mercury Return is closely conjunct his natal Sun. This indicates that in asserting himself he will be expressing his identity and individuality. This means more is at stake in any confrontation or dispute. Mars often acts as if its biological existence were on line, but here his sense of himself as an authentic person will easily feel threatened. There have been strong Sun–Mars contacts in the last two years' Solar Returns, the whole issue of self-assertion, of primitive survival and of the expression of his individuality is of major importance.

The Moon is widely conjunct the Descendant, indicating a sympathetic response in him towards others and an ability to solicit helpfulness from others. This is good for all communication with the public. It is good for his business, as his business is to do with communications.

In my most recent conversation with Jack he explained how he has been involved in redesigning all the company's notepaper and advertising. He was extremely pleased with the results, particularly their clarity and simplicity, and he believed this spoke volumes. This feels like an expression of his innate artistic ability (Venus, Sun, Neptune, Jupiter and Mercury stellium in Libra and Scorpio) made realisable by some of these planets being in a T-square in this year's Solar Return and the same planets in aspect in the Mercury Return. I had always been concerned that his work did not offer any scope for his artistically creative side but he has managed to express this in his work as well.

He also told me he is in fact a member of a prestigious gym, where they do in fact do repetitive exercises. This is an expression of both the third house stellium in his Mercury Return, and his sixth house Moon in his Solar Return. He is also running regularly and training to run in two marathons this year.

We would like to end this chapter by thanking Jack for allowing us to write about him in so much personal detail, and for supplying us with recent information about himself. We wish him well.

10

CASE STUDY ON STEFFI GRAF

Steffi Graf is one of the sporting phenomena of our age and at the age of 19 had proved herself to be in a class apart from her nearest rivals. At 13 years and 4 months she was the youngest player ever to receive a Women's Tennis Association World Ranking and by the time she was 20 she had won every major championship, including an Olympic Gold Medal.

Virtually unbeatable, Steffi combines extraordinary talent with an exceptional match temperament. During 1988 she only lost three matches out of seventy-four played and all these were when she was feeling unwell or was recovering from injury.

Despite her huge success and the tremendous amount of admiration and respect she commands, Steffi has not really been taken to the hearts of the public. This is, perhaps, partly because of her cool, matter of fact on-court personality and partly because of the ruthless efficiency with which she disposes of her opponents. It is hardly a contest at all and the result is seldom in doubt.

We chose to look at the period from Steffi's birthday in June 1988 to June 1989 because this was the time that she actually achieved her Golden Slam. She became only the fourth woman in history to win a Grand Slam, that is to hold all four major championships, the Australian Open, the French Open, Wimbledon and the US Open, at the same time. Adding to this exceptional achievement, she also won the Olympic Gold Medal, making it a unique Golden Slam.

This period is also interesting because right at the end of it, just before her next birthday, Steffi suffered an unexpected defeat in the final of the French Open, which prevented her from gaining a second Grand Slam in succession.

We will start by taking a look at the main features of Steffi's natal chart (Figure 10.1). This is, not surprisingly, a specialist's chart with the Sun, Moon, Mercury and Ascendant all concentrated in Gemini.

Tennis is, perhaps, the ultimate Gemini sport, combining quick thinking and reactions with manual dexterity, agility and fleetness of foot. It is played in short bursts of fast-moving activity which ideally suits the Geminian temperament. Great flexibility and adaptability are needed to cope with varying court surfaces, weather conditions and opponents' styles of play. It calls for the ability to access situations and other players instantly and is rather like a form of dialogue between two people. It can be summed up as a battle of wits and dexterity and thus essentially, a Mercurial activity.

The Sun in Steffi's chart is focal, being very close to the Ascendant. This shows in her strong, regal presence, dignified bearing and Leonine hair and appearance. She is every inch a queen. The Sun on the Ascendant shows someone who is used to receiving a tremendous amount of attention and who thrives on being in the limelight. But it also brings with it a feeling of being exposed, on display and of having no privacy.

There is a feeling of being special, picked out, not ordinary, not someone who can blend in with the crowd. As a person with the Sun rising, Steffi may well be the apple of her father's eye, but she is also likely to feel that a tremendous amount is expected of her and that she is always on view. This is especially true with the Sun on the twelfth house side of the Ascendant where there is a craving for privacy and to hide away. The person with the Sun in the twelfth learns at an early age to create a private world to retreat to. It is interesting to note that

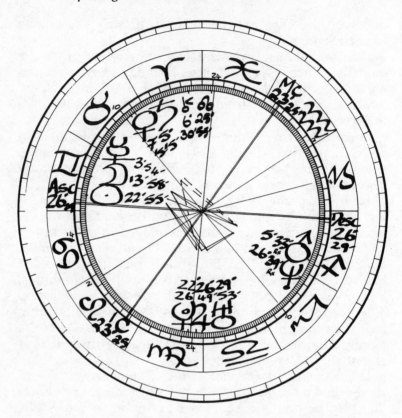

Fig. 10.1. Steffi Graf's natal chart 14.6.69, 3.40 a.m. GMT Mannheim,
W. Germany, 49°N29' 8°E29'.

with this placement there is a home movie, that has been
widely shown on television, of Steffi at the age of 3 being
coached by her father. Already, at that age, she was being
encouraged to develop her talent and being filmed doing
it. She was learning early that she was a public person and
that much was expected of her.

With a twelfth house Sun there may be some sense
of inner confusion about her identity which could well
stem from having too much attention and involvement
from her parents, so that, perhaps, she did not have the
space to just be and grow up to be herself. Because of

this her self-image may be somewhat unclear. In order to counteract this, she, like most people with a rising Sun, takes great care to present a sharply defined image. There is a need to make a statement, an impression with her appearance.

The twelfth house Sun suggests that Steffi has the ability to visualise a purpose and then simply allow things to take their course rather than trying to make things happen. She is thus able to let go and flow towards her aims. An abundance of mutable planets with no cardinality re-inforces this feeling of things happening without her actually consciously initiating them. With only mutable and fixed energy she can adapt and keep on hanging in but it is difficult for her to actually change things.

With the Moon deeply buried in the twelfth, Steffi is likely to be an intensely private person and fantasy may be an important part of her life which may make it difficult for her to sort out what she really feels.

With Mercury, too, in the twelfth, the need for privacy is further emphasised and yet, with the Sun on the Ascendant, she has put herself in the position of being permanently on display. With so much complicated twelfth house energy, she is likely to project a lot of contradictory feelings, which may explain some of the unwelcome attention she has received and her feelings of anxiety about security.

The only aspects to Steffi's Sun are the squares from the Pluto, Jupiter, Uranus conjunction. This is an intense and explosive combination of energies showing a driving need to achieve something enormous and to prove to herself that she is a uniquely powerful and successful person. Although this is coming from her, there is also a feeling that part of the need is, perhaps, to please her father, which she may feel that she can only do by being successful. If she is trying to win her father's love through proving herself to be the best, then this is likely to be a bottomless pit which no amount of success can fill.

There is going to be a tendency with the Sun square Jupiter for her not to consider her own inner needs but to drive on to achieve more in order to earn approval. But it does also show an inner faith and optimism, a belief that she will succeed in reaching her goals. There is an inherent expectation of success which gives her the ability to go for what she wants, to be daring and to take risks.

With Sun square Uranus, there is the feeling of being different, of being someone exceptional who doesn't fit in. Sun–Uranus people are often exceptionally gifted in some way that sets them apart from others. This enables them to endure tremendous isolation and gives an ability to stick uncompromisingly to their chosen path no matter what the price in personal happiness. Uranus indicates a detached, unyielding attitude and Steffi shows this in the cool, ruthless way she sweeps aside all opposition.

Steffi's power and strength show in the Sun–Pluto square. She is able to dominate and control matches through sheer strength of will as well as by her formidable skills. Opponents feel intimidated and overwhelmed by her and find it almost impossible to maintain any belief in their own ability to win.

With Sun–Pluto there is an obsessive desire to make her game perfect and to root out any faults, and Steffi imposes stringent training routines on herself in order to continually improve her performance. After winning a big match with apparently flawless tennis she will say that she plans to go and work on some aspect of her game that needs improving. Winning alone is not enough and she will push herself to the limit to become a perfect player.

The Sun–Pluto person is totally single-minded and will sacrifice everything to achieve their aims. There is a tremendous amount of self-control which often masks a fear of the chaos that might ensue if control were relinquished. Power is generally a huge issue and there is a fear of being overwhelmed which can cause the Sun–Pluto person to struggle continually to gain and keep power. Steffi is likely to feel that if she loses control then others may overwhelm her and that the only way to survive is to maintain her grip on herself and on situations.

The Jupiter–Uranus conjunction squaring the Sun signifies a perfect sense of timing, an instinctive ability to do
exactly the right thing at the right time, while Jupiter–Pluto
suggests an urge to gamble and to push things right to the
edge in order to save them. To live by her sporting talents
offers a perfect outlet for this need. Being in the position
of having to win to survive is the ideal vehicle for these
energies, which also give her the ability to pull out the
very best in herself when she is threatened. But on the rare
occasions when she is not able to pull things back from the
brink of defeat she is likely to feel utterly devastated.

Steffi has a Venus–Saturn conjunction in Taurus in the
eleventh, which indicates that there is likely to have been
a lack of warmth in her childhood, with feelings, perhaps,
not being expressed outwardly. Venus–Saturn generally
shows problems with self-worth, a feeling of not being
loved for yourself but of having to earn it. The person
with this aspect does not feel valued for what they are
but for what they do. They are likely to feel that they do
not deserve happiness and this can cause them to sacrifice
love for duty and achievement. Therefore Steffi is likely to
feel that she has to try harder and harder to become perfect
in order to earn love. But of course, success can never fill
the need to be loved simply for herself. On the contrary,
it is likely to increase any feelings of insecurity. If success
equals love, then what happens if she fails?

The reserve of Venus–Saturn shows in Steffi's unemo-
tional on-court manner. She very seldom displays any
reaction or feeling, which makes it hard for the public
to relate to her or to share in her success. Having this
conjunction in the eleventh shows that friendship, too,
may be a somewhat difficult area for Steffi and she
does tend to keep herself separate from other players
on the circuit. This, while giving her more privacy,
must also cut her off from a valuable source of support
and companionship.

Mars in Sagittarius in the sixth is symbolic of Steffi's
work. She used her energy in a pleasurable and enthusiastic way to earn her living by playing a game. It is worth

noting that with Mars in the sixth house, Steffi is often ill. She suffers a lot from colds and other minor illnesses which are likely to be brought about by the incredible strain she puts on herself and the excessive amount of work she does. Mars in Sagittarius is a buoyant and self-renewing energy but even that has its limits and at times her body rebels. Her defeats always occur when she is feeling ill and she is forced to let up on the relentless pressure she imposes on herself.

Having Mars opposite Mercury and the Moon indicates her lightning-fast reactions. It gives her the ability to think and respond quickly by immediately translating thought into action. She can also act very effectively on pure instinctive reaction when necessary.

Neptune in the sixth shows the achievement of something quite beyond the ordinary, quite magical, in her working life and also suggests that, perhaps, at some later date she may put her energy into something more spiritual or mystical. With Neptune opposite Mercury from the sixth house to the twelfth, all the other twelfth house planets, Venus–Saturn in the eleventh house and Aquarius on the MC, there is a strong pull to do something beyond the personal, to be of service to the world in general in a truly altruistic and selfless way. It will be interesting to see what path Steffi follows when her tennis career is over.

We will now take a look at Steffi's Solar Return for the period in which she achieved her Golden Slam (see Figure 10.2). The most immediately striking thing is the extraordinary concentration of planets in Gemini, which reflects her natal chart. Once again this chart is nearly all mutable and fixed with only Neptune cardinal. So Steffi was working with familiar qualities and felt comfortable and at home that year.

Working through the sequence outlined in Chapter 5, we find the Sun in the seventh house. This is an indication of a time in which interaction with others is greatly accentuated. Tennis is a seventh house activity with two people pitting themselves against each other. If

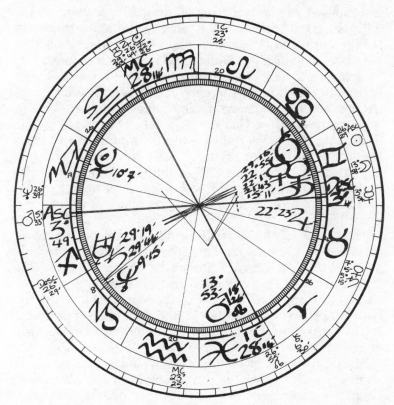

Fig. 10.2 Steffi Graf's Solar Return, 5.51 p.m. GMT, 13.6.1988, Brühl, 49°N29' 8°E29'.

one looks at the inner dynamics of playing competitively, the other person represents a challenge in which we try to push ourselves that little bit further in order to gain victory. Although the objective is to win, true satisfaction only comes from playing someone with sufficient skill to push us to perform at our very best. This is the nature of the Sun in the seventh house which needs, through its interaction with others, to strive to develop the best in itself.

With the Sun in the seventh, Steffi will have felt the need to become publicly recognised and appreciated. It is a time when she will have felt much more comfortable with her public role, so that being in the limelight was a confirmation of her identity. She needed this interaction with people in order to understand herself more fully.

Going on to look at the aspects to the Sun, we see that it is conjunct the Moon, Mercury and Venus. It is a time of fruition when everything literally comes together.

As mentioned in Chapter 2, a New Moon in a Solar Return signifies a year of exceptional importance and this was certainly true for Steffi. It was a time when she was able to put herself heart and soul into achieving her aim and successfully bringing it to fruition. Her need to shine and be recognised for her own particular genius was at a peak this year.

The period of this Solar Return will have been a major turning-point in how she saw herself and also represents a time during which her life was changed for ever. She gained what she most wanted and yet she lost her much-valued privacy. She became public property. With the New Moon echoing the one in her natal chart it is almost as though she was born afresh with her new life starting at this point.

The Sun–Mercury conjunction which is almost exact shows a peak time in the development of her Mercurial–Geminian qualities which reached new heights that year. It also shows a time in which her thoughts will have been directed inwards by all that was going on in her life. She is likely to have been going through a period of intense introspection as her outer life changed so dramatically. Her achievements will have brought about a change in the way she thought about herself and there must have been much self-questioning and self-analysis. It also signifies the change that must have taken place in her thinking as she understood the full implications of her success.

With Venus conjunct the Sun, it was a year when Steffi reaped the rewards of her efforts and actually got what she most wanted and had been working towards for a long time. Her achievement will have confirmed her identity as a uniquely gifted individual and given her a greater sense of her own value.

With such a strong emphasis on the seventh house and Venus, Steffi is also likely to have gone through a period of questioning and reassessment concerning relationships. There will have been a strong urge to become closer to others and her success in her career may have shown up a lack of close relationships in her private life.

The Sun is also widely in opposition to the Saturn –Uranus conjunction and although this has really passed out of orb by this year, it does reflect the period of preparation that went into this time of culmination. The enormous effort and concentration (Saturn) which went into the realisation of her own unique genius (Uranus). It also shows that the last few years were unlikely to have been easy and that she will have had to struggle through many ups and downs, overcoming setbacks and disappointments before she succeeded in her ambitions.

Looking at the Ascendant in Steffi's Solar Return, we see that this is Sagittarius and that it falls on her natal Mars and that the Descendant falls on her natal Mercury. In addition, it is the same axis as in her natal chart where she has Gemini rising, so this is clearly a year of great significance in her life.

Sagittarius rising shows a year of excitement and challenge when life really opens up. There is an ability to take risks and to make the most of any opportunities, combined with enthusiasm and optimism, which means that Steffi was able to approach life in exactly the right way to succeed in her aims. She was able to proceed boldly and hopefully, confident of success, which made the attainment of her goals seem an easier task this year.

She will have been looking to the future and moving on from one success to the next. This emphasis on forward momentum will have made it easier for her to concentrate on the challenge ahead rather than dwelling on what was already achieved. It was a year for bold strokes and inner faith, a year in which anything will have seemed possible.

The Ascendant ruler, Jupiter, is in the sixth in Taurus, showing all the hard work and tireless enthusiasm needed for her to meet the year's challenges. It also shows how success in her work became a concrete reality. The only aspects to Jupiter are semi-sextiles from the Sun, Mercury and Venus, which indicates that there was little distraction for her in putting everything she had into expressing herself through her work at this time.

The Midheaven is in Virgo and lies on the Uranus–Jupiter–Pluto conjunction, with the IC on her north node. The Virgo MC shows the meticulous preparation and sheer hard work which Steffi put into her career goals. Her standards will have been impossibly high and nothing less than perfection will have been good enough. No detail will have been ignored as she attempted to iron out every fault. She is also likely to have defined very clearly exactly what she wanted to achieve and to have analysed very carefully every step on the way. It is also probable that this excessive drive for perfection eventually led to her defeat in the French Open when she was not feeling well.

The Midheaven ruler in the seventh shows that Steffi sought to realise her goals through interaction and competition with others and that receiving public recognition and acclaim was an important ingredient in her motivation. Mercury is, of course, part of the four-planet conjunction, emphasising once again how everything came together that year. It is very closely conjunct both the Sun and Venus, showing how she achieved what she wanted in her career through her Mercurial skills.

We will now go on to look at the Moon in Steffi's Solar Return. This is almost exactly in its natal position, being only a degree and a half past her Lunar Return. This is further confirmation of what an exceptional year this was for Steffi. With the Moon back in its original position, she will have been feeling at home and comfortable with herself. There will have been a sense of familiarity and emotional security which made it easier to go for her solar aims and take risks. The Moon in Gemini is a restless, adaptable one so that being in a constant state of movement and changing circumstances would have felt comfortable and right for her.

Having the Moon in the seventh emphasises Steffi's greater involvement with the public that year. She came out of her twelfth house and talked more openly about herself and this will have felt more comfortable to her at this time. The Moon in the seventh also signifies her public popularity, which reached a peak during this year, with her incredible success and new openness which showed her to be a likeable and articulate person.

The Moon is square to Mars, reflecting the natal opposition between the two planets. Squares are aspects of manifestation and Steffi was able to use her instinctive skills and quick reactions to achieve what she wanted. A Moon–Mars square also reveals a time of increased assertiveness and a desire to speak out and be direct.

Working through the other personal planets, we find that Mercury, too, is back in its own sign so Steffi is thinking in a familiar mode. With Mercury in Gemini in the seventh, she is going to be learning a lot through her interactions with others. Actually competing will have taken up a lot of her mental energy and she will have gained a new understanding of herself through this. With such a strong seventh house emphasis, Steffi must surely have been thinking about personal relationships and may well have had someone in particular on her mind.

Venus, also, is part of the stellium in Gemini in the seventh and this is a very different energy from her natal Venus–Saturn conjunction in Taurus. Steffi will have been feeling much more sociable than usual and able to relate in a lighter and more communicative way. She is likely to have become aware of the lack of ordinary companionship and friendship in her life and will have felt the need to talk to people more and exchange ideas. She will have been attracted to people who made contacts easily and who were friendly and communicative.

Mars in Pisces suggests that Steffi was able to trust to life and go with the flow. It is indicative of an inner faith in one's ability to do what one wants and so she was able to let go and allow herself to float towards what she desired. As in her birth chart, where Mars is in Sagittarius, Steffi is working with mutable energy, which is the quality in which she is most at home. In addition to this, the Solar Return Mars is in the third house, which shows a particular adaptability and need for constant movement and change in order to feel alive.

A trine from Mars to Pluto in the eleventh shows that she will have enjoyed using her energy in a single-minded and totally dedicated way to achieve her dearest wish.

The combinations that form aspects in both charts are Moon–Mars, Sun–Midheaven and Sun–Uranus. The Moon–Mars aspect has already been looked at while we were considering the Moon. The Sun–Uranus has almost passed out of orb. So this leaves natal Sun trine the Midheaven, which has become a square in the Solar Return. This reflects a change from something that is a pleasurable motivating factor into the urge to make an effort to actualise the achievement of her aims and purpose in life. This is the year that she made the potential success into a reality.

Looking at the house emphasis, we can see that six planets, including the Sun, Moon, Mercury and Venus, are in angular houses and this certainly indicated a year of great activity. It was very much a time of making things happen.

Lastly, we will look at the aspects between planets and angles of both charts. There are a great many of these which further emphasises the significance of this particular time.

Perhaps the most important of these is the Solar Return Ascendant–Descendant axis falling directly on Steffi's Mercury–Mars opposition. Just how significant this aspect is can be assessed by considering the nature of her work, in which the ability to combine the qualities of these two planets so effectively is an essential factor in her success. Mars in Sagittarius is an ideal placement for someone who plays for a living. It has enthusiasm, buoyancy, optimism and a sheer joy in moving, combined with a self-renewing flow of energy. As long as it is enjoying what it is doing, Mars in Sagittarius will never get tired. So when this Mars is combined with Mercury in Gemini, which is a lightning-quick and crystal-clear thinker, which thrives on making instant decisions on the run, then you have a pretty unbeatable combination for a fast-moving game like tennis. This then is the feature of Steffi's natal chart that is being highlighted by the Solar Return Ascendant and one can see with what brilliance she used this energy as an essential part of her self-expression during that year. It was a time when she was able to propel herself forward and make a decisive impact on the world.

The Solar Return Midheaven picks up her natal Uranus –Jupiter–Pluto conjunction and she used this powerful, explosive energy to great effect in the attainment of her aims. This aspect also reflects the drastic and transformational change that her status and image went through and the fame that she achieved during the year.

It is also worth noting that the MC–IC axis also falls across her nodal axis, making this truly a year of destiny.

Now we will go on to take a look at Steffi's Mars Return for the period in question (Figure 10.3). Mars is in the ninth house, showing that Steffi had a powerful need to do things that were personally challenging to her and nothing could have been more so than winning a Grand Slam. With this placement she will have leapt at the opportunity to tackle this enormous task. With Mars in Sagittarius in the ninth there is a tremendous future orientation, so that she was able to propel herself forward, taking whatever risks were necessary to succeed.

Having Sagittarius on the MC is confirmation that Steffi's sights were firmly focused on the future and that she was taking action to achieve far-reaching goals that were meaningful to her. It is likely that this desire to be travelling towards personally significant aims gave a relaxed and optimistic approach which actually made them easier to achieve.

Through the expression of her Mars energy, she will have been wanting to project an image of faith and

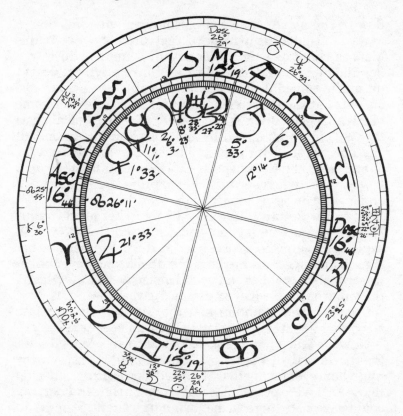

Fig. 10.3. Mars Return for Steffi Graf, 16.1.88, Melbourne, 37°S45'
144°E58'.

optimism in the way she behaved. There is a feeling
with Sagittarius on the Midheaven and Pisces Rising, of
her flowing towards her appointed destiny, rather than
being involved in any kind of conscious struggle.

With Jupiter, the Midheaven ruler, in the second, Steffi
certainly made a lot of money through her Mars energy.
In fact, it is likely that she will have been set up for life
as a result of her success at this time. Jupiter is square
the Sun and sesquiquadrate Mars, which shows that she
was able to make this success happen, to actualise it.
With Jupiter ruling both Mars and the Midheaven she

earned her money through playing, through doing what she enjoyed doing and it is almost as though the money comes as a bonus.

With a Pisces Ascendant in the Mars Return, Steffi was able to let go of any self-imposed limitations in the expression of her energy and trust that she would get what she wanted. She was able to let go and allow things to happen without trying to control things too much. This is repeating the message of Mars in Pisces in her Solar Return.

Pisces Rising also shows a high degree of adaptability. Steffi was able to change her behaviour to suit any situation and go with whatever was happening. This was a time when there were many different calls on her energy and she may have found, at times, that she lost sight of what she wanted on a more personal level where many sacrifices will have had to be made.

The Ascendant co-rulers, Jupiter and Neptune are situated in the second and tenth houses respectively, thus emphasising that she used her Mars energy to attain money and success. We have already looked at Jupiter as the Midheaven ruler but Neptune in the tenth is a continuation of the theme of Steffi flowing towards her goals, which is repeated in many different ways. Having the Ascendant Ruler in the tenth shows that her search for success and status in the world was the area through which she expressed her Mars energy. It could be said with Neptune in the tenth house that she made her dreams come true.

The Moon also in the heavily tenanted tenth shows the emotional importance of her achievements to her and, also, of course, symbolises her increased fame and popularity. Through her sporting activity she became a public figure.

A Sagittarian Moon trine Jupiter emphasises once more the buoyancy and optimism that she felt. But it is also conjunct Saturn and Uranus, showing a taut, finely balanced emotional charge and she is likely to have gone through many ups and downs in mood during the attainment of her Mars aims. This is a very stressful combination and perhaps things just became too much for her at times, bringing about the illnesses which caused her to lose. It also reflects back to Steffi's natal Mars to which the closest aspect is an inconjunct from Saturn. This shows her incredible capacity for hard work and driving need for perfection and the strain that this puts her under, making her vulnerable to illness caused by overwork and stress.

The Sun and Mercury in the eleventh house emphasise Steffi's concentration of energy and thought on future hopes. Through the use of her Mars energy she sought to enact what she wished for herself and make it real. Mercury is square to Pluto showing her single-minded mental approach to what she was doing.

Lastly we find that Venus is in the twelfth house in Pisces and square to Mars. The square indicates that Venus brought what she wanted through her own efforts and hard work, but being in Pisces in the twelfth suggests that this was, perhaps, at the price of her personal happiness and privacy.

Looking at Steffi's Lunar Return for the month that she actually achieved her Grand Slam by winning the US Open (Figure 10.4), we see that the Moon is in the tenth. As described in the chapter on Lunar Returns, this is a time when 'you feel you have arrived' and this was certainly true for Steffi. She was exactly where she wanted to be and this will have given her enormous emotional satisfaction. She will have been feeling really good about herself at this time and was also getting the public recognition she sought. It was a time of fulfilment in her professional life and standing in the world.

This message is reinforced by the square between the Sun and Moon. Solar and Lunar Returns with Sun–Moon contacts mark major turning-points and this is especially so with the square being from the first to the tenth. Her success and how she felt about it (Moon in tenth) will have brought about a change in the way she saw herself and will have strengthened her sense of identity (Sun in first). The Sun in the first house shows a need to make an

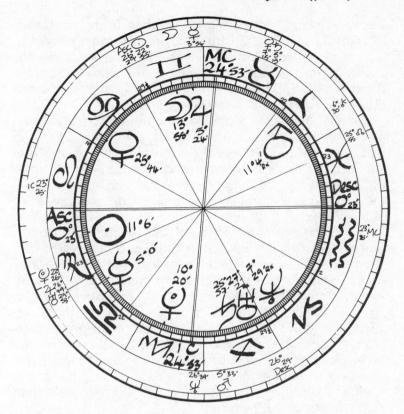

Fig. 10.4. Lunar Return for Steffi Graf, 9.34 a.m. GMT, 3.9.88, New York, 40°N40′ 73°W50′.

impact on the world and the confidence to achieve this. Achieving recognition will have been a central emotional need this month.

With Jupiter also in the tenth we have a further indication of the faith and confidence that Steffi had at this time, which enabled her to seize her opportunity and ensure success. She was aiming very high and had enough self-belief to succeed.

With four planets, including the Sun and Moon, in angular houses, this was a month of great activity. The T-square has the Mercury–Mars opposition repeated from the natal chart, except that now Mars is in Aries and Mercury is in Libra. So they are in their own elements but are now cardinal rather than mutable. It was a month of making things happen. In the Lunar Return this opposition is squared by Neptune, indicating that she used these energies to make her dreams come true.

Having Virgo rising shows the amount of meticulous preparation and care with which she approached getting what she needed. Taurus on the Midheaven shows the solidness of her achievement and also the sensible, no-nonsense image she presented to the world. It also reveals the enormous amount of emotional security invested in her professional achievements.

Finally we will take a brief look at the Lunar Return for when Steffi lost in the final of the French Open (Figure 10.5). There is once again a New Moon but this time it is on the cusp of the sixth house forming a yod with Pluto and the Saturn–Neptune conjunction. This is an extremely stressful combination of energies and it is not therefore surprising that Steffi became ill at this time. Inconjuncts often signify ill health and when you have three of the outer planets inconjuncting both the Sun and Moon, then you have something of a crisis. In Steffi's case, the illness itself was only slight, but the effect it had on her life at that time was pretty traumatic.

The fact that Scorpio is on the Midheaven and Pluto is in the tenth emphasises just how much of a crisis this was for Steffi. It must have felt as though all her power had been stripped from her and she was threatened with annihilation. This echoes the natal Sun–Pluto square in which this possibility is likely to be an ever-present fear. With Sun–Pluto, failure cannot be taken philosophically – it is a devastating humiliation.

Uranus conjunct the Ascendant shows just how much of a shock this was and how unexpected. It had been taken for granted by everyone that this would be just another routine victory for Steffi, but gradually during the course of the match it became apparent that a shock defeat was on the cards as Arantxa Sanchez enthusiastically

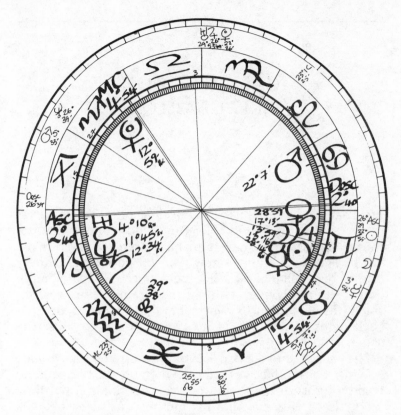

Fig. 10.5. Lunar Return for Steffi Graf 9.12 p.m. GMT, 3.6.89, Paris, 48°N52′ 2°E20′.

fought her way to victory. At the end there was almost a feeling of disbelief in what had been witnessed. Steffi herself appeared quite bemused by what had happened, as though she had lost her grip on the situation. This is not surprising with the Saturn–Neptune conjunction in the first house. The conjunction is symbolic of things falling apart and, in the first, it was her confidence and self-belief that fell apart, allowing self-doubt to creep in, so that she no longer appeared invincible but had become vulnerable and human.

11

CASE STUDY ON
ERIC CLAPTON

Eric Clapton has established himself as one of the greatest musicians in the world. His career now spans almosts thirty years, during which there have been ups and downs, but he is now enjoying a new wave of popularity, chiefly due to his brilliance as a live performer. His passionate, lyrical guitar-playing, with its inspirational improvised solos, thrills audiences everywhere and many people go back night after night as no two concerts are ever the same.

His background is no less extraordinary than his guitar-playing. His mother was only 16 when he was born and he was brought up by his grandparents, thinking that they were his parents and that his mother was his sister. His father was a married Canadian airman who went back to Canada and whom Eric has never met. At the age of 9 he discovered the truth and has often described the tremendous shock that this was to him.

Also relevant to our case study is his passionate and obsessive love for Patti, whom he first met in 1969, when she was married to George Harrison, one of his best friends. During the years of unrequited love that followed he recorded *Layla*, perhaps his most famous album, which is four sides of passionate love, longing and pain all addressed to Patti. They did finally get together but it was not to last and they separated in 1984. But he is still writing songs about the 'Old Love' that won't die. Over the years she has inspired a great many songs and it is possible to follow the story of their relationship all the way through from the songs he has written.

We have chosen to look at the period during which he played a record-breaking eighteen nights at the Royal Albert Hall, which culminated in the presentation of a concerto for guitar and orchestra, co-written by him and Michael Kamen. The three orchestral evenings were a new venture for Eric and were something of a gamble for him. In fact, they were a triumphant success, receiving a rapturous response and clearly forming an important landmark in his career.

Looking at Eric's natal chart (Figure 11.1), we can see that it is particularly rich and complex. He is someone who has fulfilled much of the potential of his chart, having explored both the heights and the depths of the natal promise.

The Sun is in Aries in the first and is part of a cardinal T-square, with Saturn in the fifth and Neptune in the seventh. This T-square, perhaps, neatly sums up his life and work. The Sun in Aries in the first shows the fire and passion, the desire to be someone and to make an impact on the world. There is a boldness of approach, an honesty and straightforwardness – he must be seen and recognised for who he is. With the Sun in Aries, there is a certain inner vulnerability and insecurity that needs to push itself forward to make sure that it is seen and recognised, in order to reassure itself that it really is someone. With the Sun square Saturn, this is greatly magnified and establishing an identity becomes a central struggle in life. Sun–Saturn people need to achieve something of significance in order to prove to themselves that they are of worth. But nothing is ever quite good enough so there is a constant drive for self-improvement. Saturn acts as a judge who assesses every achievement critically and concludes that it could have been better and Eric has said that his aim is to make every concert better than the one before.

Nothing of value comes easily with Sun–Saturn and it is through struggling with difficulty, often self-imposed,

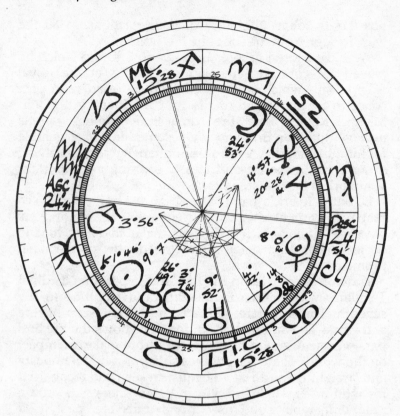

Fig. 11.1. Natal chart for Eric Clapton, 4.30 a.m. GMT, 30.3.45, Ripley, Surrey, 51°N18′ 0°W29′.

that self-esteem is painfully built. Rejecting commercial success early on by leaving the Yardbirds at the height of their popularity, Eric has often said that he never wanted hit records, only to be a good musician. He has started again many times during his life in his quest to build up something that was meaningful to him.

With the Sun square Saturn there is a tendency to underestimate his own skill and he has said of his playing, that it is not cleverness but just feeling and has described it as channelled instinct, which is a perfect description of the Sun in Aries square Saturn in Cancer, but it is one that leaves out the enormous amount of skill that it takes to translate the feelings so powerfully into an art form.

With Saturn as the focal point of a cardinal T-square, there is a driving need to prove oneself by achieving something worthwhile in life and with it in the fifth, it is through his creativity that Eric has sought to do this.

The last planet in the T-square is Neptune in Libra in the seventh. This opposition to the Sun shows a fundamental conflict between the necessity to develop a sharply defined identity (Sun Aries first) and the urge to transcend the limits of his individual ego and experience a dissolution of boundaries, a loss of self in order to merge with the greater whole. Eric manages to actualise this potential through his music when his inspirational playing transports whole audiences to another plane. Eric himself has described this experience as time standing still, while he goes into a trance and people go with him. He said on *Desert Island Discs* that 'There is nothing better on earth than being in a concert situation where you can take a whole audience out of themselves, even for just a moment. When two thousand people just leave themselves it is a joyous, a great gift.'

This is perhaps a perfect description of his Sun–Neptune opposition when it is operating at its highest level. With this T-square he has taken his pain and suffering and distilled into an art form of exquisite beauty, with which he can uplift and inspire others. It is a very healing energy, both for him and for those who share the experience.

Eric appears to have lived his Sun–Neptune opposition at all levels, starting with the confusion over his identity and his absent father; then, perhaps because of this, he has a tendency to idealise others – he has many blues guitarist heroes – and he, himself, is in turn idealised by others. There is the intense unfulfilled longing and his past escapism through drugs and drink. It also describes his gypsy life-style as a musician and the spiritual yearning that drives him onwards in search of an ideal and this is an image that he strongly identifies with, often referring to himself as a wanderer.

The Sun does, in fact, form an aspect to all four outer

planets showing the universality of his appeal. He represents something beyond the individual and is able to
express himself in a way that vast numbers of people are
able to identify with.

Here is another quote from Eric which illustrates how he
experiences this powerfully aspected Sun. Talking about
improvising in front of an audience, he says it is 'a real
discovery of your inner resources and that's what my
character is all about and my playing is all about. To get
up there and just go inside and draw out something that
makes you feel good first and foremost is not something
that happens every night. I have to consciously become
unconscious.'

The Sun–Uranus sextile, which is very close, emphasises
the desire to realise his potential as a unique individual
and create his own place in the world. Uranus in the
third indicates that he has done this through his ability
to communicate in a way that is distinctively his alone.

Having Pluto trine the Sun shows the pleasure he
obtains from plunging into his own depths and bringing
what is deep and hidden into the light. It shows the
powerful self-renewing energy that thrives on crisis and
can rise from the ashes many times.

The Moon in Eric's chart is in Libra in the eighth
opposite Mercury in the second. The Moon in the eighth
shows the richness and depth of feeling which draw
him into intense and deeply transforming emotional experience. An eighth house Moon is one of the factors
illustrating his capacity to go through the pain of years
of unrequited love for Patti. With this placement it is
intensity of feeling that is sought and even extreme
emotional suffering seems preferable to the emptiness of
not feeling.

Having the Moon in Libra and opposite Mercury suggests that Eric may be uncomfortable expressing his
feelings on an intimate personal level, but shows how
well he can communicate them through the more abstract
medium of music and song. With the words of his
songs and through his guitar-playing, which is almost

conversational in style, he talks with graphic intensity about how he feels. The opposition to Mercury shows an ability to stand back from his feelings and analyse and describe them. With Mercury in Aries, he does this in vivid, passionate imagery. Mercury in the second shows that this talent is a valuable resource for making money.

Mercury is also conjunct Venus, which shows that Eric is likely to be thinking a great deal about love and relationships and that it is important for him to communicate these thoughts as this helps him to sort things out in his mind.

Venus in Taurus in the second shows the sensuous, luxury-loving side of Eric, with his passion for Ferraris, expensive clothes and beautiful models. Money may not have been a motivating factor for him, but he will certainly have enjoyed spending it!

As has been shown by his continuing love for Patti, with Venus in Taurus square Pluto, Eric's feelings do not change easily and he tends to love obsessively. With this combination, love is likely to be all or nothing: there are no half measures with Venus–Pluto. A sextile from Saturn to Venus adds further confirmation of the endurance of Eric's feelings.

Venus–Pluto, like the Moon in the eighth, prefers even extreme pain to the emptiness of not loving at all. There is an enormous intensity of feeling which means that love inevitably brings suffering and, through this, trans-formation. With Pluto in the sixth and Venus in the second, Eric has been able to use this suffering in his work, so that his pain has become not only a means of self-expression but also a source of income. Layla is a beautiful example of all the longing, pain and feelings of powerlessness experienced by a Venus–Pluto person in love.

Venus is also involved in a yod with Mars and Neptune. There is a very close sextile between Venus and Mars with Neptune inconjuncting both. This aspect pattern reveals the yearning for a perfect and wonderful relationship that is quite out of this world. It also shows someone who can inject a touch of magic into everything they do and who appears irresistibly mysterious and attractive to others. Eric is likely to be able to make those he loves feel that they are very special to him, and, indeed, he is able to do this with whole audiences. With Neptune in the seventh, he has a gift for making each individual feel personally blessed by his love. This is one of the qualities that elicits the extraordinary loyalty of his fans.

This yod makes it hard for him to accept the ordinary, everyday realities of life. There is a constant restless yearning for a beautiful ideal and a continuing attempt to bring this about, which causes much dissatisfaction and suffering. This drive to realise an ideal vision comes to fruition in his work, where for brief periods he is able to create moments of perfect beauty.

This inner restlessness reflected by the yod and intensified by a square from Uranus, means that, as he says himself, his personal life is always complete chaos and that as soon as things become content he always does something to upset the apple-cart. He describes this as subconcious and something that he does not have any control over. People with Mars in Pisces or in aspect to Neptune often have this feeling of their own actions being outside their control and something they are not responsible for. This is doubly so when Mars is in Pisces and in aspect to Neptune!

With Mars rising square Uranus, Eric is likely to be somewhat autocratic and to feel that he is a law unto himself. In an interview with *Q* magazine he described himself as 'an isolated, cold, rather intimidating, generally selfish person to be around'. This sounds like a pretty accurate description of this combination. It also reveals the sharply self-critical nature and courageous honesty of Mars rising and the somewhat arrogant 'take me as I am' attitude which is likely to antagonise others and lead to conflict.

Mars square Uranus is completely uncompromising and Eric has always done his own thing, refusing to pander to musical fashion or to court popularity. It is this integrity which has led to the second flowering of his career in the late eighties.

With Mars–Uranus, Eric generates an electric sexual energy and a close sextile between Mars and Venus enhances this charismatic attractiveness and softens the sharpness of the Uranus contact, making him seem more approachable and accessible.

A trine from Saturn to Mars gives some stability and reflects Eric's pleasure in working hard. He enjoys being busy and with the trine being from the first to the fifth this is through expressing himself creatively.

Aquarius rising shows Eric's general friendliness and his orientation to group activity. He is likely to feel at his best when he is participating in co-operative activities with others, so that working with groups of like-minded musicians and giving out to large numbers of people will suit him perfectly.

This rising sign also confirms the very strong need for freedom illustrated by many other factors in his chart, which includes the Sun in Aries, Mars rising square Uranus conjunct the IC and Sagittarius on the Midheaven. He is going to need to feel that he is unconfined and free to do whatever he wants. Aquarius rising also lends detachment and Eric is able to stand back and talk about himself in an objective way. Having the chart rulers, Saturn and Uranus, in the fifth and third respectively denotes that his self-expression is focused through his ability to develop his creative talent and communicate in an original way.

Sagittarius on the Midheaven shows the necessary faith to aim really high and get there. It also signifies Eric's capacity to take risks and to gamble with his career by trying new things. There is also a tremendous future orientation, Sagittarius does not dwell in past success but moves ever onwards looking for new challenges. With a Sagittarian MC, Eric is going to be very adaptable in his aims and how to achieve them. There is a lot of optimism and buoyancy which means that if something does not work he will just try something else.

Jupiter, the MC ruler, is in the seventh, reflecting the huge popularity Eric has achieved. He gives of himself very generously and because of this receives back vast amounts of public love – it is a two-way flow. His audiences also feel that he acknowledges and appreciates them, which increases the goodwill towards him.

With Jupiter in the seventh, people tend to expect an enormous amount of him. They expect to be transported out of this world at every concert and this is quite a lot to live up to. However, with Jupiter here and in Virgo, Eric conscientiously sets out to fulfil these expectations. There is a strong need to be of service and to feel useful and Eric serves his public well. There is something self-effacing and humble about Jupiter in Virgo and Eric is often to be found playing in the background on other people's records, often without acknowledgement.

Jupiter is unaspected which gives it a rather unpredictable on/off quality and Eric is likely to be subject to sudden bursts of unbridled enthusiasm. As Jupiter is his Midheaven ruler, it indicates that his career is likely to be subject to ups and downs which may seem to be outside his control. It also explains, along with the Sun–Neptune opposition, the 'Clapton is God' syndrome of the sixties. It is easy to project God onto someone with an unaspected Jupiter in the seventh, which indicates that adulation is likely to get out of hand at times.

On a personal level, Jupiter in the seventh signifies someone with enormous expectations from close relationships and this is greatly exaggerated by having Neptune there as well. There is a tendency with Jupiter in the seventh to look for happiness through other people and to feel let down and disillusioned when they do not provide it. Yet there is also a need to be completely free as well and Jupiter in this house finds in hard to be tied to one person, as it searches for meaning and self-knowledge through its interactions with others.

To end this look at Eric's natal chart, we will consider the implication of Uranus on the IC. Planets on the IC are very significant as they underpin everything else. With Uranus here we have someone who, to quote his own words, has led 'a detached and lonely life' and whose 'whole life has been based on doing things on my own'.

Uranus on the IC describes the unusual circumstances in which Eric grew up and that he had a father whom he never saw. He has talked about feeling different as a young child but not knowing why. It also shows the tremendous shock it was for him when he learned the truth about his mother and grandparents at the age of 9. He says that his shock lasted well into his teens and that it changed his whole outlook and even his physical appearance. He adds that it was from this point that he felt a complete lack of identity. Uranus on the IC shows that he must have felt as though the ground had been cut from under him and this sense of being disconnected and rootless has driven him to lead the restless, nomadic life-style of a musician. This early shock must have made it very hard for him to feel secure or to trust people and he may get very anxious when he gets close to someone, fearing that something terrible will happen to destroy his happiness. To put it in his own words, 'If everything is going well, I panic, wondering when it's all going to go wrong.'

This then is the base from which he is operating and he has forged his identity afresh through developing his own unique skills. His playing is something that is his alone and it gives him a great sense of security and he has described it as his haven, his strength, his friend.

Going on to look at Eric's Solar Return for the year which culminated in his triumphal orchestral concerts at the Royal Albert Hall (Figure 11.2), we see that the Sun is in the sixth conjunct Venus and Mercury and square to a stellium in Capricorn.

Having the Sun in the sixth means that this has been a year of very hard work for Eric and he will have been focused almost entirely on his working life. His commitment and effort will have drawn on his deepest creative sources, making them more accessible and enabling him to utilise them in an external way. It is interesting to note that with the Sun in the sixth this year,

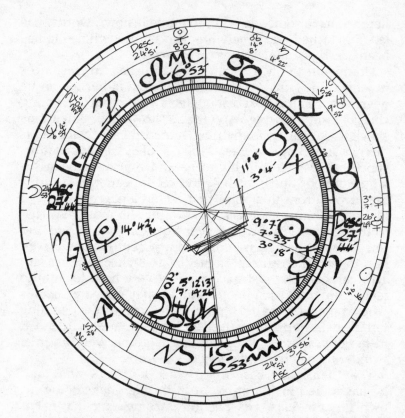

Fig. 11.2. Solar Return for Eric Clapton, 8.10 p.m. GMT, 29.3.89,
Cranleigh, Surrey 51°N9' 0°W30'.

he released an album called *Journeyman*. The dictionary
definition of a journeyman is a workman who has finished
his apprenticeship, so Eric has chosen to identify with
the sixth house image of a skilled worker. To most of us
the word journeyman suggests a travelling craftsman and
this ties in, not only with the squares to the stellium in
Capricorn in the third, but also back to his natal Jupiter
in Virgo, for which 'Journeyman' is, perhaps, the perfect
description.

It may have been a time of working too hard, of ignoring
other needs and of driving himself on in a way that could

have drained and depleted him. It would have been a good time for him to look at this and try to work out a balance which ensures that his working routines serve his inner needs. It would also have been beneficial for him to think about how he looks after himself and perhaps learn to develop a healthier more self-caring life-style.

The Sun in the sixth can also be a time of healing, so it is likely that through the realisation of his creative purpose, Eric will have experienced a sense of becoming more integrated and of healing some of his early wounds.

The Sun conjunct Venus in a Solar Return generally indicates a time of increased sociability and pleasure with an emphasis on relationships. But with this conjunction in the sixth house, it is likely to be working relationships that were in focus and he is likely to have been sociable in the context of his working life. With the Sun and Venus being the rulers of the angles, this year is likely to have marked a turning-point in his relationship to the public and seen a noticeable increase in popularity. Sun–Venus, too, shows a desire to please and it will have been important to Eric that people liked him. He will have wanted to give pleasure to others and with this conjunction in the sixth, this would naturally have been through his work.

As with Steffi Graf, the Sun–Venus conjunction brought Eric what he wanted and he described the success of his orchestral concerts at the Albert Hall as a 'dream come true'. This success is likely to have changed his relationship to himself, confirming his identity and enabling him to value himself more.

With Mercury also conjunct the Sun and Venus, Eric spent a lot of time giving interviews and talking about himself. This is likely to have encouraged a process of reassessing himself which will have continued all the time and the events of the year will have given him a new perspective and understanding of himself. With this triple conjunction, there was an even greater ability than usual to put himself over well and this increased the public esteem and affection in which he is held.

These three planets are square to a stellium in Capricorn which contains the Moon and also Neptune and Saturn, which are the two other planets involved in Eric's natal T-square with the Sun. This then is a year in which the promise of the T-square was actualised – the dream came true. As with Steffi, this is a year when everything is brought together.

The square between the Sun and Moon shows this year to be a significant turning-point in Eric's life, one that will stand out as a time when important changes were made. There will have been some degree of internal struggle as he sought to bring his feeling nature and his identity together and this is likely to have brought many things to the surface. This inner tension will have increased his creativity and the two principles are likely to have come together in his work, giving him a new sense of wholeness.

In order to become more himself he will have needed to break away from self-defeating emotional patterns and let go of the past. To achieve this he will have had to change old habits and relinquish some of the things that have made him feel comfortable and secure in the past.

The Sun–Saturn square confirms that this was a year of very hard work when Eric put a great deal of effort into achieving his aims and getting what he needed for himself. He is likely to have felt a strong sense of commitment to himself and his work and will have put a lot of energy into making sure that everything was done perfectly, if not better! This aspect is repeated from his natal chart and re-emphasises his innate Saturnian qualities and struggles.

Years with Sun–Saturn aspects are also periods of re-evaluation so it may have been a time when Eric had to look at how he was living his life and assess what was working for him. It is a time for shedding things that are no longer relevant and for reorganising areas of life that need changing. He will have had to examine any self-limiting patterns of behaviour which may have been preventing him from becoming who he wants to be.

This aspect also signifies a year when life is taken very seriously and Eric will have had to do a lot of organising and dealing with practical matters. With Uranus and Neptune also involved, it is likely to have been quite a chaotic time, with lots of frustrating setbacks and delays.

It may have been quite a strain holding things together as there is likely to have been a tendency for arrangements to fall apart just when they seemed to be running smoothly.

Uranus square the Sun indicates a time when nothing can be counted on. Things tend to happen out of the blue and there is a sudden burst of activity followed by an unexpected difficulty. Eric will have experienced a sense of urgency about making changes and getting things done and yet is likely to have come up against many frustrating obstructions. However, there will also have been periods of manic activity when everything had to be done at once and an enormous amount of ground was covered.

A year with Uranus aspecting the Sun is always a time of far-reaching change and for finding a new direction in life. There is an openness to fresh ideas and the confidence to act in an original and independent way. Eric would have been in exactly the right frame of mind to try something different and it may even have led to the discovery of a new path in life. The square in the Solar Return reflects the natal sextile but now there is a more urgent drive to actualise the natal potential. This aspect will be even closer in his 1990 Solar Return so we may expect even greater changes then. This two-year period is a time for getting in touch with his own uniqueness and for discovering exactly what he wants from life, what his own individual purpose is. It is also a time when his need for freedom will have been exaggerated and he is likely to have swept any restrictions away quite ruthlessly.

Neptune has been square to the Sun in Eric's Solar Returns since 1985 and was closest to exact in 1987 and 1988, so this has been a long period of intensification of the restless, yearning quality of the natal Sun–Neptune opposition, of the actualisation of the natal promise, realising the dream.

This will have been a time of letting go and of learning to trust and to flow with life. Any rigid structures or concepts will have dissolved, leaving Eric free to make more conscious choices in the future.

Years with Sun–Neptune aspects are generally very creative times, with inspiration flowing freely and this period has marked the resurgence of Eric's career and the new wave of popularity.

Although these three outer planets individually form aspects to the Sun in other Solar Returns, this is the only year that they all do. This makes it a particularly significant time as all these energies combine with the Moon to square the conjunction between the Sun and Venus, which also rule the angles, indicating that this really is a time of fruition.

Having these planets in the third forming squares to the sixth shows what a restless year this is likely to have been for Eric. It will have been one of constant work and being on the move, rushing from one thing to another.

The last aspect to the Sun is a sextile from Mars, which illustrates the energy and confidence with which Eric was able to tackle life. He will have known exactly what he wanted and will have been able to act swiftly and decisively to achieve it. His courage and boldness will have been emphasised so that it will have been easier for him to make sweeping changes and try new things.

Moving on to the Solar Return Ascendant, we see that it is in Libra and that it lies on Eric's natal Moon with the Descendant on natal Mercury.

Libra rising shows a year with much social interaction, when shared experience becomes an essential route to self-discovery. Eric has worked with many different people during the year and will have gained a new perspective on himself through this. He is likely to have found great pleasure and satisfaction from co-operating with people on special projects, such as composing the concerto with Michael Kamen. There will have been a need to seek out people who shared his ideas and interests and, with the Ascendant ruler in the sixth, this, once again, is likely to have been through his working life. In this very work-orientated year, it is not surprising that the main focus of his self-expression would be through his work. With the Solar Return Ascendant being trine to his natal Ascendant he will have experienced an ease of expression this year. He would be moving forward in a familiar mode. The Ascendant ruler being in Aries, his Sun sign, also confirms this ease of self-expression.

Leo on the Midheaven marks a significant year in the realisation of Eric's creative goals. It will have been a time when it was particularly important to him to shine and be recognised for who he is and he will have been seeking to put over an image worthy of admiration and respect. With the MC ruler, the Sun, in the sixth trine the MC and conjunct Venus we are, once again, drawn back to work and this indicates that long-term rewards would be realised through Eric putting himself wholeheartedly into his work. This he has done, thus fulfilling the task of the year and reaping the rewards.

Going on to the Solar Return Moon, we see that it is in Capricorn which underlines the importance of work and shows Eric's emotional involvement in achieving his goals. This is a year when practical considerations and career aims are more important than personal needs. He will have sought emotional security through achieving position and status and is likely to have been more reserved and cautious than usual about emotional involvements with people.

With the Moon in the third house, there will have been a strong need for mental stimulation and Eric will have been emotionally bound up in his ideas. It will also have accentuated his need to communicate his feelings, reflecting the Moon–Mercury opposition of the natal chart. It is likely that through this many memories will have been brought to the surface and he will have been able to reassess past experiences and understand his emotional needs better.

The Moon square Mercury emphasises this tendency and brings a more concrete urge to communicate his feelings. This aspect corresponds to the opposition between the planets natally with the square making the urge to express his feelings even more compulsive. He certainly talked about himself a lot during the year, reflecting on his past experiences and how he felt about them. This is likely to have helped him to make sense of them by talking them through and there will have been a lot of self-analysis going on.

Eric's mind will have been especially alert and responsive to new ways of seeing things. His thinking will have been very imaginative and it will have been a good year for creative writing.

A square from the Moon to Venus indicates that this may have been a difficult time for emotional relationships. Inner conflict between his feeling responses and his relational needs will have caused feelings of dissatisfaction. Because these feelings have been forced to the surface this year it will have been a good time to work through these problems, in order to try to resolve them.

With an inconjunct from Jupiter to the Moon, some stress may have been caused by the rapid expansion in Eric's life. The huge success and the enormous expectations are likely to have caused him to feel rather insecure and anxious at times.

The Moon is conjunct Uranus and this means that Eric is likely to have experienced some kind of shock that jolted him out of habitual emotional patterns. It may have been a time when he experienced a reconnection with painful feelings that he had previously cut off from, which will have led to a greater emotional connectedness and grounding.

It will have been a year of unpredictable happenings and excitement and Eric is likely to have felt very hyped up and restless and it may have been very difficult for him to rest or even slow down.

Personal freedom will have been a big issue for him as he will have felt very claustrophobic if people tried to pin him down too much. He is also likely to have been very impulsive in his behaviour, rushing off to do things as soon as he thought of them.

This is likely to have been a year of important changes in Eric's emotional life as he became more consciously aware of the effect that past experiences were having on his present behaviour and it marks an important turning-point in his self-awareness.

The Solar Return Moon is trine Eric's natal Venus, showing that he will have been especially warm and affectionate in his responses to people that year and this will, in turn have attracted a favourable response from others. It indicates a time of increased popularity and inner happiness.

The Moon is also sextile natal Mars, showing that Eric's feeling responses were likely to have been more highly charged than usual and that it may have been easier for him to express anger and assert himself.

We will now go on to take a brief look at the other planets in the Solar Return Chart.

Mercury is in its natal sign of Aries, showing once again that this was a time of ease in self-expression for Eric and being in the fifth house this was also a very creative time for him. With Mercury fifth square Uranus third he will have had fun playing with new ideas and his mind is likely to have been buzzing with them this year. With this combination it is not surprising that he embarked on a radically different creative project like co-writing and performing a concerto. Mercury being also conjunct Venus reflects the softer, more lush musical bias of this lyrical orchestral piece. There is also a sextile from Mercury to Jupiter showing Eric's desire to expand his horizons and do something bigger and more mentally challenging. Something outside his normal field of operations.

Venus in Aries is a very different energy to his natal Venus in Taurus and it is likely that in his relationships Eric will have been more outgoing and volatile and that love may have been more abstract and less physical for him. With Venus, the chart ruler, being part of the triple conjunction in the sixth and square to the stellium in Capricorn, it is likely that Eric will have poured most of his love into his work and will not have had much time for personal relationships. Venus in the sixth house generally signifies someone who is in love with their work.

Mars in Gemini is operating in the same mutable mode as Eric's natal Mars in Pisces, but he will be much more mentally orientated and precise. He will have been very clear about what he wanted to do and able to see clearly the best way to go about it. With Mars in Gemini in the eighth, Eric will have plunged into working on his ideas with great intensity and would have had access to deeply buried feelings and resources, which he will have been able to express with great clarity. Mars is inconjunct to the Saturn–Neptune conjunction in the third, showing how he was able to actualise his ideas and visions – make his dreams come true. It also shows that he is likely to have been under a great deal of strain and that this must have been a physically exhausting time for him, which could have taken a toll on his health.

Jupiter in Gemini in the eighth emphasises the pleasure and enthusiasm with which Eric will have plunged himself into writing and communicating and the success that this brought. Jupiter in the eighth symbolises the discovery of buried treasure and Eric is likely to have gone on an inner journey and unearthed great riches.

There are a great many aspects between Solar Return planets and natal planets, showing this to be an exceptional year. We have already looked at those to the Moon so we will go on to consider those to other personal planets in the Solar Return chart. The Solar Return Mercury is opposite natal Neptune, showing this to be a year when Eric will have been particularly imaginative and inventive. He will also have been exceptionally intuitive and receptive, picking up on everything that was going on around him and being able to tune in to other people's thoughts. This is an ideal aspect for co-operating with others on musical projects.

The Solar Return Mercury is also square to natal Saturn, indicating a more serious and concentrated way of thinking and bringing some discipline and purpose to the imagination and inspiration of Neptune.

Natal Neptune is also opposite Solar Return Venus which, as mentioned in Chapter 5, is for creative artists an especially inspirational time when artistic sensitivity is at its most refined. It is also a year of being exceptionally tuned in to the public appreciation of beauty, making this a commercially successful time also. This was certainly true for Eric this year, for, although these things normally apply to him anyway they were especially emphasised during this period.

There are also an exceptional number of aspects repeated in the Solar Return from the Natal Chart. We have already talked about the Sun aspecting the planets from the natal T-square and also about the natal Moon–Mercury opposition now being a square. It is interesting to note that both oppositions in Eric's natal chart have become squares in this Solar Return.

The Solar Return Moon is conjunct Uranus, which is much more compulsive than the natal sesquiquadrate and Eric's restless emotional nature will have been greatly exaggerated this year, so that it is likely to have been a time of frenetic activity and emotional ups and downs. It is also likely to have been a year of increased insight into his habitual behaviour patterns, enabling him to move away from past conditioning and experiences.

The natal Mercury semi-square to Uranus, too, has become a square indicating an increase in the drive to actualise this aspect.

Mercury is conjunct Venus in both charts, but in the Solar Return it is closer and both planets are now in Aries. This will make its expression more passionate and outgoing and at the same time more abstract, lending itself well to creative fantasy.

The Venus–Mars sextile from the natal chart is also repeated, showing Eric's attractiveness to be emphasised this year and that the balance between the two principles remained the same.

The natal sextile from Venus to Saturn has become a square in the Solar Return showing a more urgent need to earn professional respect for his work in addition to public popularity.

The natal inconjunct from Venus to Neptune has also become a square, enabling this romantic yearning to be more concretely expressed and showing this to be a very creative time.

Lastly, we will look at the natal planets that are on the Solar Return angles. As in Steffi Graf's case, the Ascendant–Descendant axis in Eric's Solar Return falls on an important natal opposition.

Eric's Solar Return Ascendant picks up the Moon–Mercury opposition, which signifies his ability to express his feelings, which has always been such a vital part of his success. It is this inherent talent for communicating exactly what he feels, in a way that millions can understand and identify with, that has made him so hugely popular. The honesty, openness and vulnerability which he reveals, both in his work and in interviews, make him seem much more accessible and human than most stars. It is this quality that sets him apart from other performers and gives his public the feeling that they actually know him. This is the feature being picked out by the Solar Return Ascendant, making it even more pronounced this year and, in addition to his concerts, Eric did many more interviews than usual in which he talked very freely about himself. With the Ascendant on his natal Moon, Eric would have been very much in tune with the public, with the mood of the moment, and this will have drawn a favourable response.

With natal Mercury on the Solar Return Descendant, communication with others was emphasised this year and Eric would have been able to put his ideas over clearly, to express himself well and be listened to.

The Solar Return MC falling on natal Pluto shows the enormous risk that Eric took in putting on so many concerts at the Albert Hall, which culminated in the untried venture of performing with an orchestra. This was an enterprise that could have ended in triumph or disaster. Perhaps Eric felt the need to put his power to the test and prove something to himself and to the world. It ended in total success, his power as a performer confirmed and his popularity vastly increased.

We will now take a look at Eric's Venus Return for the year in question (Figure 11.3). We chose the Venus Return for Eric because of the prominence of the Venus principle in his life and work.

Venus is in the tenth house and conjunct the Sun, re-emphasising that this was a period when Eric's relationships were likely to have been focused around his career and what he wanted to achieve in life. Love would have been bound up with his sense of identity and creative powers, so that professional achievement and public love will have been more important to him than personal relationships. Through his achievements he will have gained a greater sense of who he was and will have learned to love himself more as a result. Success will have brought great personal happiness and helped to heal some of the wounds in his self-esteem.

With Venus in the tenth trine to Uranus in the fifth, we can see that it was through using his own special creative talents and expressing them in his own individual way that Eric achieved his aim. It was through being appreciated for the uniqueness of his particular gifts that he sought happiness this year. As there are no more aspects to Venus it suggests that he will have wanted a lot of space and freedom this year and that he may have found it hard to combine personal relationships with his working life.

Having Venus conjunct the Sun in a Venus Return shows that this was a very important time in the development of Eric's sense of identity. Through the expression of his Venusian energies and the success that this brought, he will have gained a clearer sense of who he was and of his purpose in life.

Aries on the Midheaven indicates that, in the way he

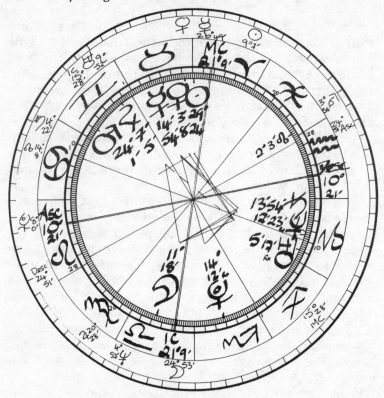

Fig. 11.3. Venus Return for Eric Clapton, 11.30 a.m. GMT, 19.4.89, Cranleigh, 51°N9′ 0°W30′.

related to the world, Eric was wanting to put over an image of independence and self-reliance and will have wanted to be appreciated as a sharply defined individual.

Mars, the Midheaven ruler, in the eleventh shows that it was actually through group activity that he strove to do this. The eleventh is the house of our hopes and wishes for the future and with Mars here, Eric was taking action to make these a reality. Mars is exactly trine both the natal Moon and Ascendant, showing the ease with which he was able to do this. The only aspects to Mars in the Venus Return are sextiles to the Sun and the Midheaven, underlining the concentration of Eric's energy on achieving public recognition and appreciation.

The MC–IC axis falls, like the Solar Return Ascendant, on Eric's Moon–Mercury opposition, confirming the importance of this aspect in his success during the year. With the Venus Return MC on natal Mercury and the IC on natal Moon we have further evidence that it was his ability to communicate his feelings and share his past experiences that helped him to achieve his goals, increase his public standing and become more popular this year.

With the Venus Return Sun also being on natal Mercury and opposite the natal Moon, it shows just how powerfully and openly he was able to do this at this time. The Venus Return IC on the Natal Moon suggests that his past was more accessible to him this year and that he was able to go deeper into his early memories and understand them better. It will have been an important time for him on a personal level in helping to heal some of the wounds that could make relationships a painful issue for him.

The Venus Return Ascendant is in Leo, which is the natal Descendant and it is conjunct his Solar Return Midheaven, while the Ascendant ruler is conjunct both Venus and the Midheaven, all of which emphasises what a very important year this was for Eric in his relationship to the world and to himself.

Having Leo rising and an Aries Midheaven in his Venus Return, shows that Eric is going to want to be seen as giving out love in a generous, passionate way, both personally and in his career. A Leo Ascendant in a Venus Return indicates an open-hearted generosity in his relationships with others. It also shows the creative way in which he expressed his love and that this brought him the admiration and respect that he was looking for.

With the Venus Return Ascendant on natal Pluto, Eric made a tremendous impact and this stresses, like the Solar Return MC on natal Pluto, that Eric was really laying himself on the line by taking on such an enormous and risky project. But in this case it was his personal relationship with the world that he was risking. It could have backfired and then he would have lost public love rather than gaining it.

The Moon is in its natal sign of Libra and is opposite Eric's natal Sun, while the Venus Return Sun is opposite his natal Moon, giving additional confirmation of the significance of this particular time. These aspects show that Eric is likely to have been deeply affected emotionally by the effect he had on his audiences. They also suggest that he may be addicted to the high he gets from this,. so that he is left with a huge hole afterwards which is difficult to fill. Ordinary companionship may seem flat and boring afterwards and yet the Moon in Libra does have a very strong need for everyday human companionship.

The Moon in Libra in the third in a Venus Return reflects once again the continuing theme of Eric's need to communicate and share his feelings with others. It is square to Saturn–Neptune in the sixth, showing that he actualised this in his work through effort and inspiration. It also shows that he may have experienced quite a lot of loneliness and isolation as a result of his work and through being constantly on the move. It is also square to Uranus, carrying on the Moon–Uranus theme from his natal chart and Solar Return.

With Mercury in Taurus in the tenth, Eric would have been thinking in a very practical way about love and relationships and his thoughts would have been firmly fixed on getting these needs met through his career. With Mercury opposite a fourth house Pluto, Eric will have been thinking a lot about past relationships and much that was deeply buried will have come to the surface, changing his thinking in a fundamental way. This aspect also shows the powerfully transformative effect that he will have had on others through his communicative skills.

We took Eric's Lunar Return for the month of the Albert Hall concerts (Figure 11.4), and, appropriately, this happened a few hours before they began.

It is worth nothing first that once more there is a Sun–Venus conjunction. This has appeared in both the other return charts but this time it is almost exact. So this then marks the time, with the conjunction in Capricorn, that

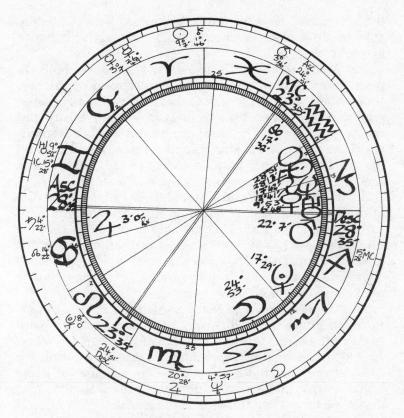

Fig. 11.4. Lunar Return for Eric Clapton, 1.55 p.m. GMT, 18.1.90, Cranleigh, 51°N9' 0°W30'.

Eric actually got what he wanted. It became real; the dream came true.

The Moon in the fifth shows this to be a time when Eric was emotionally focused on his creative output and self-expression and this is the emphasis of the month. In practice, he probably did little else this month but rehearse and perform and will have enjoyed the feeling of being completely immersed in doing what gives him most pleasure.

Eric will have been feeling very comfortable with his role as a creative artist and performer and will have derived emotional security from this. He has said that the Albert Hall feels like home to him, so he was literally at home in a place of entertainment. Perfect fifth house Moon symbolism!

The Moon in the fifth also shows that his ability to perform and entertain brought him increased popularity. It describes, too, the nature of what he was actually doing, which was to express his feelings in a creative way and indicates that he was in tune with what the public wanted, which, in turn drew a good response. As he has Cancer on the fifth house cusp in his natal chart this represents a peak time in the development of an inherent quality.

As in the Solar Return, the Moon is square to the Sun–Venus conjunction, showing this to be an important turning-point for Eric. He was able to bring his creative impulses and his feeling needs together to achieve a greater wholeness. The success he attained will have changed the way he felt about himself, enabling him to love himself more.

The Moon is sextile to Mars, showing that he was able to act effectively to get his emotional needs met and with Mars in the sixth, this was, of course, through his work. Having Mars on the Descendant indicates a month of great activity around lunar matters and a time of lively and dynamic interaction with others. Mars angular also denotes a time when things actually happen. With Mars in Sagittarius, Eric was able to bring energy and enthusiasm to what he did and act in a free and unihibited way. He will have had faith in his ability to get what he wanted for himself and would have felt that he could do anything.

The Moon is trine the Ascendant, as it is in his natal chart, and conjunct the Solar Return Ascendant and this underlines what a time of exceptional ease it was in the expression of his feelings. There was an easy flow between the inner and the outer. The Moon is also trine the Midheaven, making it part of an air Grand Trine, which illustrates Eric's pleasure in communicating and in feeling mentally connected to people.

Having Gemini rising in a Lunar Return, with Mercury, the chart ruler, in the seventh, accentuates a very familiar theme which is prevalent in Eric's natal chart and all the returns – namely, his ability to communicate his feelings. With Gemini rising this month it is immediate and comfortable. It would have been a time when he will have wanted to talk a lot, write a lot and, of course, express himself through his guitar-playing. Having Mercury in the seventh conjunct Neptune and Uranus shows the inspirational genius with which he was able to do this.

With Jupiter on the Ascendant, Eric will have been feeling very confident and optimistic. Any anxieties or doubts that he had about the concerts will have vanished as soon as they began. He would have been putting so much positive energy out that he was bound to succeed. Jupiter rising shows the enormity of the expectation and how important it was to him to succeed on a personal emotional level. He dared to hope for too much and got it. Jupiter is also sesquiquadrate Pluto in the sixth, emphasising the hugeness of the project he had taken on and what an enormous gamble it was.

The Sun–Venus conjunction in the eighth inconjunct the Ascendant is a further indication of this. The inconjunct describes the stress and anxiety that must have accompanied the venture. But Sun–Venus in the eighth, like Jupiter rising, Moon in the fifth and Mars on the Descendant, point to the drama and passion of Eric's emotional self-expression at this time. He will have been in exactly the right mood to take on a big challenge.

Jupiter is opposite to Uranus and this falling across the Ascendant–Descendant axis shows the inspired genius that Eric displayed and reveals that he instinctively chose the perfect time to risk presenting a new enterprise. It also shows his ability to electrify and awaken people, stirring up hidden feelings by his performances. It suggests, too, that he may have become aware of some of his own deeply buried inner needs.

The Lunar Return Midheaven is closely conjunct the natal Ascendant, showing the great significance of this particular month in Eric's development and expression of his natal potential. In fact, this Leo–Aquarius axis is represented on the angles of all the charts, which does emphasise the importance of this particular period in Eric's personal growth.

With Aquarius on the Midheaven, Eric was aiming to bring down the barriers between different kinds of music and to present his own unique style in a new setting which opened things up. It was a far cry from the purist blues attitude he held in the sixties.

The Midheaven rulers, Saturn and Uranus, are in the eighth and seventh respectively, with Uranus being conjunct Mercury, the Ascendant ruler. It always marks a significant time when the rulers of the angles come together and this is reflected, too, in the Solar Return where the rulers are conjunct.

With the ruler of the Midheaven in the seventh and eighth, we can see that this was a time of intense emotional interaction with others. The Midheaven in a Lunar Return shows our emotional aims for the month, so Eric would have been seeking to increase the emotional bonds between himself and his public and his ability to do this effectively brought him increased success in his career.

With Neptune back in the seventh, where it is natally, and conjunct Mercury, Eric was able to put himself over in an even more inspired and seductive way than usual, keeping his audiences completely spellbound. The feeling for everyone was one of sharing an experience. His Neptunian quality of drawing people in and involving them was heightened at this time, so that, although it was his dream that came true, his audience felt part of the dream rather than merely spectators.

At the time the concerts were taking place, the progressed Moon in Eric's Solar Return was conjunct his natal Neptune, showing this to be the moment for the dream to come true.

The Astrological Association is the main co-ordinating body in British astrology and has an international membership. Benefits of joining include Annual Conference, London Research Conference, meetings and seminars, journals and specialist newsletters and data section. Further information from: Enquiries office, PO Box 39, North PDO, Nottingham, NG5 5PD.

The Urania Trust is an educational charity. It owns the Astrological Study Centre, 396 Caledonian Road, London NI IDN (Tel. 071 700 0639), which houses the joint libraries of the Faculty of Astrological Studies, the Astrological Association and the Astrological Lodge of London, and the Astrological Association's bookshop. It acts as an information service and has up-to-date details on other teaching organisations and the many groups of astrologers throughout Britain.

The Association of Professional Astrologers is a recently formed organisation for professional astrologers. Further information from: Jacqueline Knapp Tupholme, 49 Nassau Road, London SW13 9QG.

COMPUTER SERVICES
AND ASTROLOGICAL
ORGANISATIONS

Computer Services

Adam Scott, 9 Priory Woodway, Huntington, York YO3 9JH. Tel. 0904 651234

AstroAdvice Bureau, Darrington Lodge, Springfield Road, Camberley, Surrey GU15 1AB. Tel. 0276 21739 Fax 0276 61730

Jupiter Invitations, 48 Berrans Avenue, Bear Cross, Bournemouth BH11 9BT. Tel. 0202 572194

Spica Services, Flat 1, 42 Highcroft Villas, Brighton, Sussex BN1 5PS. Tel. 0273 562910

Star Chart Analysis, Rock Place, 34 Cowl Street, Shepton Mallet, Somerset BA4 5ET. Tel. 0749 342943

The Astrology Centre, 60 St Stephen's Street, Edinburgh EH3 5AL. Tel. 031 225 2779

Astrological Organisations

The Faculty of Astrological Studies is a teaching body founded in 1948. The Faculty runs correspondence courses at beginner, intermediate and advanced levels; seminars and classes in London and Bath; annual Summer Schools at Jesus College, Oxford and Counselling Courses for Astrologers. The Faculty Diploma is internationally recognised. Further information from: The Registrar, BCM Box 7470, London, WCIN 3XX. Tel. Haywards Heath (0444) 453504.

BIBLIOGRAPHY

Arroyo, Stephen, *Astrology, Psychology and the Four Elements*, CRCS Publications, California, 1975
——*Astrology Karma and Transformation*, CRCS Publications, California, 1978
Binnington, Dianne, *The House of Dilemma*, Snowhite Imprints, Bristol 1981
Carter, Charles, *The Astrological Aspects*, L. N. Fowler, Essex, 1977
Coleman, Ray, *Survivor: The Authorised Biography of Eric Clapton*, Futura Publications, 1985
Cunningham, Donna, *Being a Lunar Type in a Solar World*, Samuel Weiser, Inc., Maine 1982
Filbey, J. M., D.F.Astrol.S., *Calculation of Solar and Lunar Returns*, Faculty of Astrological Studies, 1976
Greene, Liz, *Saturn*, Samuel Weiser, Inc., New York 1976
——*The Astrology of Fate*, George Allen & Unwin, London 1984
——*Star Signs for Lovers*, Arrow Books Ltd, London, 1980
Hand, Robert, *Horoscope Symbols*, Para Research, Massachusetts, 1981
——*Planets in Transit*, Para Research, Massachusetts, 1976
International Tennis Federation, *World of Tennis*, published annually by Willow Books
Jackson, Eve, *Jupiter*, Aquarian Press, Northamptonshire, 1986
Koestler, Arthur, *The Sleepwalkers*, Penguin Books, 1964
Lilly, William, *Christian Astrology*, Regulas
Lonsdale, William, *Star Rhythms*, North Atlantic Books, 1979
Lunsted, Betty, *Astrological Insights into Personality*, Astro Computing Services, 1980
——*Transits – The Time of Your Life*, Samuel Weiser, New York, 1980

Marks, Tracy, *The Astrology of Self-Discovery*, CRCS Publications, Nevada, 1985
——*Your Secret Self*, CRCS Publications, 1989
Merriman, Raymond A., *The Solar Return Book of Prediction*, Seek-It, Michigan, 1977
Rudhyar, Dane, *The Pulse of Life*, Shambhala, 1970
Ruperti, Alexander, *Cycles of Becoming*, CRCS Publications, Washington, 1978
Sasportas, Howard, *The Twelve Houses*, Aquarian Press, Wellingborough, 1985
Tierney, Bil, *Dynamics of Aspects Analysis*, CRCS, Nevada, 1983
Tompkins, Sue, *Aspects in Astrology*, Element Books, 1989